GARLAND STUDIES IN

ENTREPRENEURSHIP

edited by

STUART BRUCHEY
ALLAN NEVINS PROFESSOR EMERITUS
COLUMBIA UNIVERSITY

T0347738

WOMEN ENTREPRENEURS

DEVELOPING LEADERSHIP FOR SUCCESS

SANDRA J. WELLS

Routledge
Taylor & Francis Group

LONDON AND NEW YORK

First published 1998 by Garland Publishing, Inc.

2 Park Square, Milton Park, Abingdon, Oxon OX14 4RN
711 Third Avenue, New York, NY 10017, USA

First issued in paperback 2016

Routledge is an imprint of the Taylor & Francis Group, an informa business

Copyright © 1998 Sandra J. Wells

All rights reserved. No part of this book may be reprinted or reprod-
uced or utilised in any form or by any electronic, mechanical, or other
means, now known or hereafter invented, including photocopying
and recording, or in any information storage or retrieval system,
without permission in writing from the publishers.

Notices
Practitioners and researchers must always rely on their own experience and
knowledge in evaluating and using any information, methods, compounds, or
experiments described herein. In using such information or methods they should
be mindful of their own safety and the safety of others, including parties for whom
they have a professional responsibility.

Product or corporate names may be trademarks or registered trademarks, and are
used only for identification and explanation without intent to infringe.

Library of Congress Cataloging-in-Publication Data

Wells, Sandra J., 1949–
    Woman entrepreneurs : developing leadership for success /
Sandra J. Wells.
        p.   cm. — (Garland studies in entrepreneurship)
    Includes bibliographical references and index.
    ISBN-13: 978-0-8153-2891-9 (hbk)
    ISBN-13: 978-1-1389-8725-8 (pbk)
    1. Women-owned business enterprises—United States—Case
studies. 2. Businesswomen—United States—Case studies. 3. Self-
employed women—United States—Case studies. 4. Entrepreneurship—United States—Case studies. 5. Success in business—United
States—Case studies. I. Title. II. Series.
HD2344.5.U6W45   1997
338.6'42'0820973—dc21

                                                              97-31034

Dedication

This work is dedicated to my husband, Bruce, and to our children, Robert, Bruce, and Christopher, who have supported me through the entire process of completing this work. Their voices were full of love and encouragement. I could not have completed this dissertation without their help.

I also dedicate this to my mother, Ricardina Lozano Omlie, whose voice contributed to my development and knowing. Her loving encouragement, her always being there when I needed her and her belief that I can do anything has helped me to become who I am today.

I also dedicate this to the memory of my father, Austin Peter Omlie, whose voice told me I was a special little girl. He was a wonderful father. He taught me that the world is within my reach.

And, I dedicate this to my brother, Colonel Austin Richard Omlie, and to my sister, Rica Rose Omlie. Their voices blended with mine in childhood and we still listen to each other with love today.

Contents

Acknowledgments

A special thank you to Dr. Ron Shearon for his faith and confidence, encouraging me to "get focused; I know you can do it." I will always be indebted to him for his support and help. He never gave up on me.

A special thanks you to Dr. James Valadez for his long-distance coaching on this project. His suggestions were of great value.

A special thank you to the rest of my committee for their willingness to work with me. Living in Texas and finishing my degree in North Carolina presented some unusual challenges and they all helped me out graciously.

A special thank you to Susan Bennett, who demonstrated what it truly means to be a helper and facilitator of the learning process. She went above and beyond to help me with the logistics of being a long-distance student.

And a special thank you to the eighteen women who contributed their time and shared the stories of their lives with me. Without their willingness to participate and their openness and honesty, I would not have been able to complete this dissertation. It was an honor to have met them all.

Women
Entrepreneurs

I

The Study

INTRODUCTION

Female entrepreneurs represent a rapidly growing element of corporate America, as evidenced in The National Women's Business Council's *1991 Annual Report* to the President of the United States and Congress:

> •By the year 2000, women will own fifty percent of U.S. businesses.

> •Women-owned businesses are the fastest-growing segment of the small business population, increasing three times faster than businesses started by men.

> •Between 1982 and 1987, gross receipts of women-owned businesses almost tripled, far exceeding the rate of growth of business receipts in general.

> •Women-owned businesses employ over three million people and report a payroll of over eleven billion dollars. (p. 1).

Given that so much of the business of America is composed of organizations started and run by women, a sobering statistic presented in the same report attests to the failure rate of these businesses: women-owned businesses fail at a rate seven to eleven percent higher than businesses owned by men.

Part of the reason for female entrepreneurial failure can be attributed to the lack of capitalization and under-expansion due to insufficient funds (NWBC 1991). However, part of the failure can also be traced to a lack of management skills (Diffley, 1983, Cuba, Decenzo, and Anish, 1983, Ibrahim and Goodwin, 1987). A 1979 Presidential Report entitled *The Bottom Line: UnEqual Enterprise in America* cited that a limited amount of management and technical training was available to "fast-track" women into the marketplace; by 1988, the situation had not changed as reported in Congressional hearings on the growth of women-owned businesses (Pinson and Jinnett, 1992). It has been found that female entrepreneurs tend to use more "leader- centered" approaches as they get their businesses off the ground (Schwartz, 1976). They tend to make most decisions themselves as they provide structure to their organization, to develop relationships with customers and suppliers, and to allocate their personal resources to start their businesses. As their organization matures, it is important that they expand their repertoire of leader behaviors to demonstrate not only concern for task and production, but also concern for people (Blake and Mouton, 1964, Hersey and Blanchard, 1968). This leadership definition may be further expanded to include challenging the process, creating a shared vision and enrolling their organizational members in the vision, enabling others to act, setting the example, and encouraging the heart (Kouzes and Posner, 1987). It also includes the personal growth and development of the leader and creating the environment for growth and development in her organization. How do women entrepreneurs learn to lead? This study explored how these women learn and how they learn to lead.

BACKGROUND

Effective leadership has been cited as a critical factor in organizational performance (Katz and Kahn, 1978, Blake and Mouton, 1986, Sayles, 1993, Mintzberg, 1990, Bennis and Nanus, 1985, DePree, 1989, Block, 1987). In many organizations, efforts to increase leadership skills of organizational managers and potential leaders have resulted in the establishment of corporate-sponsored executive and management development programs and the human resource development staffs to manage these programs and the management succession process. In these organizations, someone has staff responsibility for developing the training and learning projects for others in the organization. Corporate dollars are allocated to the training and development function and time resources are allowed for on-the-job learning.

Smaller organizations, including many owned and operated by women entrepreneurs, often do not have the staffing or financial resources to support these types of leadership development programs. There is no staff person to whom the planning and organizing of learning projects can be delegated. How do the leaders of these organizations engage in learning and developing their leadership skills? What resources do they use?

From the field of adult education comes the possibility that these leaders take personal responsibility for their learning and direct their own learning activities. Manz and Manz (1991) state that, given the rapid rate of change and growth of knowledge in today's world, people must acquire skills on their own. Adult educators have long maintained that learning be used to improve oneself: Knowles advocated the continued learning of adults to adapt to technological change, to avoid obsolescence, and to apply knowledge effectively in the midst of change (1970). Critical to understanding the belief that adults can continue to develop their skills and competencies to adapt to change is a belief that the adult learner is capable of determining and executing her own learning agenda. Motivation and initiative are important attributes of the adult embarking on the path to learning and growth, for the individual is the driver in the process of learning.

The noted adult educator Malcolm Knowles proposed a model for adult learning that recognized those adults who diagnose their own learning needs, identify resources to acquire the knowledge, and initiate learning activities. Knowles called it "self-directed learning" (1975). This recognition of individual motivation to engage in learning endeavors is consistent with Allan Tough's model of the adult learner who deliberately plans a learning project undertaken to gain certain definite knowledge and skill and who is the decision-maker of learning and the learning process (1967, 1979).

Self-directed learning has been identified as a natural learning process for adults, a process in which they are continuously engaged (Confessore, 1992, Tough, 1979). The process of self-directed learning occurs when the individual adult learner becomes aware of a "need" or "gap" in their knowledge, develops a strategy or plan (however rudimentary) to fill the need, gains the knowledge, and then uses that knowledge in the context of their everyday life. Reflection and application are key components in the learning process. The learner takes responsibility for determining his or her need and meeting it. Actual execution of the learning activities can be conducted alone or with others. Knowles (1975) acknowledged that diagnosing needs, formulating goals, and choosing and implementing appropriate learning strategies, as well as evaluating learning outcomes and establishing a learning climate, were stages of the self-directed learning process.

It is important to note that for some adult educators, all learning is self-directed learning, for no one can make someone else learn. As Carl Rogers pointed out in *On Becoming a Person*, "I have come to feel that the only learning which significantly influences behavior is self-discovered, self-appropriated learning . . ." (1961).

Adult education is not the only field that has acknowledged the essential role of self-directed learning in the life of adults. The world of management, leadership, and organizational studies has now recognized the importance of individual learning and its relevance in the corporate arena. Self-directed learning has been identified as a managerial competency for creating and sustaining the leadership required in the dynamic learning organizations of the future (Morgan, 1988, Kouzes and Posner, 1988, Senge, 1990, Peters, 1987). The "learning organization" described by Senge (1990) identifies core learning disciplines essential for organization performance: Personal Mastery, creation of a Shared Vision, Team Learning, the development of Mental Models, and the use of Systems Thinking. Each discipline requires self-initiative, personal drive to increase knowledge and skill, and the ability to learn new processes. Learning organizations respond quickly and innovatively to challenges and engage in continuous learning through the learning of their members.

Personal Mastery, the discipline of personal growth and learning, is closely related to the precepts of adult lifelong learning. Individuals continually "expand their ability to create the results in life they truly seek" (p. 141). People with a high level of personal mastery live in a "continual learning mode." They are aware of their incompetence, create a vision of what they want, and then engage in the learning that changes the current state. It is a "lifelong discipline." (p. 142).

Senge, in a presentation at the May 1992 opening sessions of the national conference of the American Society of Training and Development, spoke to the importance of learning and organizational effectiveness. He identified four cornerstones to understanding learning. The first cornerstone is that the learner learns only what the learner wants to learn. The second is that "we learn by doing." The third essential for understanding learning is that "learning is a very interesting process where you move back and forth between a world of action and a world of reflection." The fourth and last cornerstone is that within all people is the intrinsic motivation to learn. The cornerstones assist in understanding new ways of learning in our organizations, including learning how to lead.

Gareth Morgan in *Riding the Waves of Change* (1988) echoes the theme of leader self-directedness in learning. Leaders must become "competent at becoming competent" (p. 170) and develop a process for developing strategy-driven competencies in their organizations. They must take a nurturing, facilitating, coaching role to ensure the organization is equipped to make changes. The effective leader of the 90's does this by focusing on his/her own development through self-diagnosis, self-development, self-review, self-renewal, and by being open to learning and learning to learn. These are the same sets of learnable behavioral-foci and cognitive-focused skills that Manz uses to describe "self-leadership," the foundation of leading others to lead themselves (1991).

Bennis and Nanus (1985) maintain that if the leader is seen as an effective learner, others in the organization will emulate the model. Thus, the leader and the organization "nurture each other, guiding the process of creative self-discovery by which each learns how to be most effective in a complex and changing environment." (p. 205).

For Senge, Morgan, Peters, Kouzas and Posner, Bennis, and Nanus, the effective leadership competencies include building relationships with others in a nurturing, facilitating, coaching manner. These skills are identified in feminist literature as characteristic of a feminine leadership style. Astin and Leland suggest the emphasis on the values of caring, responsibility to others, empowerment, interdependence, collaboration and collegiality is integrated in the practice of organizational leadership by women (1991) to produce a model of feminine leadership that is more participative than that practiced by males (Rosener, 1990, Helgesen, 1992). This model of leadership supports the integration of home and work life as connected parts of the person's being as well as the integration of the woman being connected to those around her. It is by being connected to those around her, by forming relationships that women develop (Gilligan, 1982). Women ground their descriptions of how knowledge is gained and opinions formed in terms of listening and speaking -- the voice (Belenky, Clinchy, Goldberger, Tarule, 1986).

The metaphor of the voice applies to the many aspects of women's experience and development. Belenky et. al., found that women repeatedly used the metaphor of voice to depict their intellectual and ethical development; and that the development of a sense of voice, mind, and self were intricately intertwined (p. 18). Further, the ear registers subtle changes in tone of voice; the ear requires closeness between subject and object, and, unlike seeing, speaking and listening suggest dialogue and interaction. The voice, then, represents a mode of communicating information. The women's way of leading emphasizes the role of voice over vision, the commonly used business metaphor for a company's target (Helgesen, 1992). The woman leader's voice is a means both for "presenting herself and what she knows about the world" (*Ibid.* p. 224). It is through the voice that the woman leader accomplishes her vision: the voice is the means to the end.

Astin and Leland, in their study of accomplished female leaders (1991), identified three elements of feminine leadership: collective action, passionate commitment, and consistent performance. Collective action is the leadership process of working with and through people. Passionate commitment is the strong commitment to change. Consistent performance is initiating change by identifying problems and developing the strategies to transform the system. It involves developing networks, working together, clarifying values, listening to and empowering others, and "doing one's homework" (p.158). They rely on self-awareness and on interpersonal and communication skill. How does the woman develop self-awareness? How does one practice interpersonal communication skill? How does one build networks? How does one learn to work together? The answer may be in the listening to the "different voice" of female experiences.

PURPOSE OF THE STUDY

It is believed that learning is a natural part of adult life (Knowles, 1972, 1975, Lindeman, 1926, Knox, 1977, Bruner, 1966). Adults engage in formal learning activities for a variety of reasons: to accomplish clear-cut objectives, to engage in social contact and satisfy a need for activity, and to seek knowledge for its own sake (Houle, 1961). Adult learning can take a variety of forms: formal coursework at a college or university, on-the-job training, county extension programs, informal classes offered through a variety of community or social agencies, sports training, language training, and self-help programs, just to name a few. Learning is ever present and is essential for the development and enhancement of the self. One cannot develop fully as an adult with having engaged in learning (Rogers, 1961).

Given this theoretical foundation of the nature of adult learning, this research explored the phenomenon of learning for a select group of adult learners, a group of successful female entrepreneurs. What do they learn and how do they go about their learning endeavors? By examining learning as described by these women, this research provided insights to the ways women learn, the activities they engage in for their learning, the resources they utilize to carry out their learning, and the content of their learning.

Prior to the research, it was expected that the successful women in this study might engage in learning projects to enhance their skills as leaders. It has been found that women entrepreneurs often lacked the skills needed to be successful (Pinson and Jinnett, 1992, Ibrahim & Goodwin, 1987, Diffley, 1983, Presidential Report, 1991 and 1979). How did these women gain the knowledge needed to successfully lead and operate their businesses?

Research on women's development has postulated (Belenky, Clinchy, Goldberger, Tarule, 1986, Gilligan, 1982) that women's development is heavily influenced by their relationships with others and that they learn through connectedness with others. How do these models of women's development relate to learning patterns of the women entrepreneurs of this study? If these women fit these models of women's development, learning by "listening to voices," whose voices do they listen to?

Learning from experience has been established as a fundamental construct of adult education (Knowles, 1970, Lindeman, 1926). For women employed as managers in formal organizations, among the primary methods of learning are experiences that involve learning from significant others (Van Velsor and Hughes, 1990). It is expected that through the interviewing research method, this study will identify the learning experiences that have relevance and are recognized as significant in the lives of these self-employed women.

The literature of the female entrepreneur paints a portrait of a woman who is highly motivated, initiates action and activity without direction, and who has a high internal locus of control and achievement motivation (Bowen and Hirsich, 1986, Neider, 1987). These descriptors also have been used to describe the self-directed learner, a type of adult learner (Knowles, 1975, Candy, 1991). A self-directed learner is one who is motivated by the need for esteem, a desire to achieve or the need to grow. Not unlike other learners whose experiences are used as a rich resource for learning, these adult learners initiate their own learning activities and uncover the resources to satisfy their need for information by themselves. Their learning is undertaken to solve a problem or accomplish a task. It was anticipated that this research would support a belief that the entrepreneurs studied would fit the model of adult learner typed as a "self-directed learner."

These initial assumptions, then, guided the development of the following research questions.

What do female entrepreneurs learn and why?
How do they learn? How is this demonstrated?
What methods or processes do they use?
What resources do they rely upon for their learning?
How do they describe their learning?
What factors affect their learning?

METHOD AND PROCEDURE

This research employed a naturalistic inquiry approach that utilized qualitative techniques. Qualitative research methodology has been supported in the literature as an appropriate and congenial way to study the field of the world of entrepreneurial women (Stevenson, 1990, Moore, 1990) and the area of self-directed learning (Brookfield, 1984, Spear and Mocker, 1984, Candy, 1991).

The naturalistic approach was selected for this study based on the appropriateness of the methodology to explore the research objectives. Unlike the positivistic approach which focuses on the empirical and objective analysis of discrete and preselected variables derived *a priori*, the naturalistic researcher observes, documents, and interprets the attributes, characteristics, and meanings which comprise the focus of study. The naturalistic researcher is concerned with identifying those characteristics that make a phenomenon what it is as these characteristics emerge from the research study.

The naturalistic approach addresses a "slice of life." That is, the phenomenon being studied is examined from the viewpoint of the subject. The phenomenon is documented and represented through the natural language of the human being studied: how does she feel, what does she know, how does she know it, and what are her concerns and understandings (Candy, 1991)? In this approach, the researcher is the instrument used to examine the phenomenon and gather information. The "human instrument" can adapt to the variety of realities that are encountered in the research setting. This means that the line of inquiry can be adaptive to the responses and other cues of data as they emerge. The researcher must constantly evaluate, assess, and monitor the research process and make changes accordingly--which is not usual in a structured, quantitative approach (Lincoln and Guba, 1985, Merriam and others, 1983).

The researcher conducts the research in a natural setting for the subject studied. It is not conducted in a laboratory or rigidly constructed environment. Based on the assumptions that "human behavior is related to the context in which it occurs" and that phenomena of study "take their meaning as much from their contexts as they do from themselves" (Lincoln and Guba, 1985, p. 189), the researcher conducts the inquiry in the field setting.

In this study, data were primarily collected by use of intensive oral interviews, conducted in an open-ended, unstructured format. The interview followed the model developed by Louise Spindler (1970) called the Expressive Autobiographic Interview (E.A.I.), in which the interviewee responded to a question posed to generate a life story response, an autobiography describing the individual's experience, perceptions and values. This interview followed the language and logic of the person's thought; the interviewer intervened primarily to ask further questions in order to clarify the meaning of a particular response. This study utilized the same assumptions as Gilligan's work on moral development: the way people talk about their lives is of significance, and the language that they use and connections they make reveal the world they see and in which they act (1982).

Additional data were collected through observation of unobtrusive measures: coverage in local newspapers, scrutiny of indicators at the place of business, personal observation of the women in other settings, such as Entrepreneurial Association and Women's Chamber of Commerce meetings.

Data collection and analysis occurred simultaneously; that is, while still in the interviewing phase of the research, the researcher examined the content of each transcribed interview record. A technique of constant comparison between categories of information derived from the transcribed notes allowed for trends to emerge. Analysis of initial interview data that occurred while the data collection process was progressing allowed the researcher to expand on an initial question set and provided for further exploration with subsequent interviewees. Member checks were conducted with each interviewee prior to the conclusion of the interview: the researcher reviewed in summary the main points covered in the interview with the subject and gained agreement to the summary.

The theoretical conclusions of this study were derived from a grounded theory approach, that is, theory that was discovered or generated from data rather than abstract or tentative theory. Grounded theory is developed by entering the research without a hypothesis, describing what happens as discovered through the research process, and formulating explanations as to why it happens on the basis of observation (Bailey, 1982). Hence, no hypotheses were formulated beforehand to be either proved or disproved; theory emerged from the data collected.

Eighteen women entrepreneurs, owners of Texas, U.S.A. businesses, were interviewed for this study during the period of June through December, 1993. The women subjects are leaders of organizations with no less than ten employees, and had organizational gross receipts of $1,000,000 or more per year. These criteria were established in order to select participants who were leading and managing established, successful businesses. These women were identified through their inclusion on the "Largest Women and Minority Owned Business Lists" of the *Austin*

Business Journal and the *San Antonio Business Journal*. Four of the women were identified through the snowball effect (referral for inclusion by another participant).

LIMITATIONS OF THE STUDY

There are several factors that limit this study:

●Successful women entrepreneurs (like other successful business people) face time constraints. There was a limit to the amount of time that was made available by the women entrepreneurs. All but two women who were asked to participate in the study did agree to meet and did provide at least sixty minutes; most of the interviews took ninety minutes.

●It was recognized that an ideal location to conduct the interview would be in the subject's work place to provide an opportunity to gather many data points about the interviewee (i.e. unobtrusive measures). Comfort and the ability to give uninterrupted time was paramount to the success of the study, so other locations were sought for the interviews as well. In those cases, every effort was made to secure a quiet meeting place; however, seven of the interviews were held in noisy, impersonal cafes where hearing was sometimes difficult.

●Personal bias on my part as a researcher who has consulted to organizational leaders on leadership and organizational effectiveness issues might have skewed follow-up questions to lead to particular answer set. Any inclination to offer "assistance" to any of the women who described situations was studiously avoided.

●The findings from a qualitative study may not be generalizable to the broad population but reflect perceived reality for the group of women interviewed.

SIGNIFICANCE OF THIS STUDY

Small business research reveals that female entrepreneurs want more information to accommodate their lack of work experience and educational backgrounds related to their new endeavors (Nelson, 1987). Basic business administration knowledge is critical to organizational effectiveness as are the leadership competencies needed to provide direction to the firm and a vision of the future to both organizational members and members of the firm's external environment (customers, suppliers, lending institutions) (Greiner, 1972).

Although the need for training for entrepreneurship has been established (Zeithaml and Rice, 1987, Schwartz, 1976, Bates, 1983), the typical response of adult education has been to establish training programs in formal education settings. These may not be suitable for the schedules of female entrepreneurs or the women may not be aware of these training opportunities as sources of knowledge (Schwartz, 1976, Nelson, 1987). The results of this study provide insight into the suitability and utility of formal leadership programs for women entrepreneurs in the context of the women's attitudes and attendance in such programs. Through the results of this study, adult educators who specialize in leadership and management development may be able to plan and provide programs that meet the "pull" approach we might expect the self-directed learner to utilize.

At a minimum, adult educators can assist female entrepreneurs in the identification of resources for self-development. Hiemstra suggests information networks (1987) as a resource to provide information for learning; increased availability of self-paced learning or computer-designed learning programs may be another resource possibility.

By examining the current state of learning for this target group, a customer-oriented focus is employed to determine how we can best assist this customer and contribute to her success. Arthur Lipper III, Chairman and Editor-in-Chief of *Venture* Magazine, in his address to the 5th Annual Creativity and Entrepreneurship Council in 1988, (Solomon and Winslow, 1989) stated that the community benefits when an entrepreneur succeeds. Expanding on that concept, the societal status of women and our national economy will benefit if the members of this entrepreneurial group succeed. It is expected that the results of this study will provide information to adult educators and those who provide educational services to women business owners to better plan delivery of services.

It is also anticipated that the results of this study will provide insight to those who study the ways women learn and create their lives' work, thus expanding what we know of the feminist perspective of the world.

DEFINITIONS OF TERMS

The following terms are operationally defined for clarity in the presentation of the research.

> *Learning:* a qualitative shift in how a learner views or thinks about a person, situation, idea, experience, event, or other phenomenon of interest, addressing what is learned rather than how much is learned. It entails an interactive relationship between new ideas, experiences, and insights and existing frames of reference. (Candy, 1991)

> *Lifelong Learning:* learning on the part of people of all ages and from all walks of life using the multiple learning resources of society to learn whatever they wanted or needed to know. (Cross, 1981)

> *Self-directed learning:* process in which individuals take the initiative in designing learning experiences, diagnosing needs, locating resources, and evaluating learning. (Knowles, 1975)

> *Female entrepreneurs:* women who establish new businesses. (Dyer, 1992)

> *Leadership skills:* leading by caring, making intuitive decisions, not relying on organizational hierarchy, having a sense of work as being part of life, putting labor where love is, being responsible to the world, recognizing that bottom line should stay at the bottom. (Roddick in Helgesen, 1990); a process by which members of a group are empowered to work together synergistically toward a common goal or vision that will create change, transform institutions, and thus, improve quality of life. (Astin and Leland, 1991)

Voice: a metaphor used to depict the intellectual and ethical development of women (Belenky, Clinchy, Goldberger, Tarule, 1986).

SUMMARY

This study explored how women entrepreneurs, the fastest growing segment of American business, engaged in learning and how they learned to lead their organizations. Current models of leadership portray the effective leader as a person who practices lifelong learning, self-direction, and builds nurturing relationships with others to achieve a common goal. It is essential that the female entrepreneur enhance her leadership competencies in order to be successful in the dynamic, fluid world of change. As a vitally important business group, women entrepreneurs need to acquire and/or enhance their leadership abilities in order to direct their organizations and successfully meet the challenges of complex and rapidly changing work environments.

Through the use of the in-depth taped oral interview and review of documents, this ethnomethodological study investigated the way a group of female entepreneurs learn how to lead their businesses: why and how this learning occurs, and what factors may influence or correspond to this learning process. The focus of the study was to gather the participants' perspectives through the use of an autobiographical approach that yielded a highly personal description of the learning phenomena for this group.

The importance of this study for both those who engage in entrepreneurial studies and those who are interested in adult education lies in determining how this critically important segment of the business community develops and enhances its leadership competencies. The manner and method of how these women learn, the resources they use to gain information and self-development, and the role of learning in their lives can provide insights to how their needs may be better served. This study will also increase the body of knowledge accumulated thus far in women's studies.

Additional data around the application and uses of self-directed learning may hold insights for professional groups and associations. Chapter Two will discuss findings in the literature that support this research study.

II
Review of the Literature

INTRODUCTION

Key concepts to the understanding of how female entrepreneurs learn and acquire leadership development skills are grounded in the fields of adult education, women's studies, and entrepreneurial studies. This chapter presents an overview of the research literature examining the process of adult learning, feminist research, research involving female entrepreneurs and their practice of leadership, and the use of qualitative research approaches to examine these areas.

ADULT LEARNING

Practitioners and theorists in the field of adult education continue to seek definition and understanding of the phenomena of adult learning. Lifelong learning, formal education, continuing education, workplace learning, distance learning, self-directed learning, transformative and emancipatory learning are terms which attest to a field that is trying to explain the phenomenon of how adults learn through a variety of methodologies. And, as if categorizing and classifying the different ways in which adults learn isn't enough of a conundrum, debate continues as to whether adult learning is a process or a product and whether self-direction in learning is either a process or a product (Candy, 1991). This literature review on adult learning will examine the literature that defines adult learning, how adult learning is accomplished, and examines what adult learners learn.

One of the first theorists to contribute to the definition of adult learning was Eduard C. Lindeman. He laid the foundation for systematic theory about adult learning through his perceptions on how adults learn (1926). He emphasized the importance of experience as the resource of highest value for the adult learner. "If education is life, then life is also education" and that experience is the "adult learner's living textbook." (1926 p. 9-10) He expands the relevancy of experience and learning:

Adult education is a process through which learners become aware of significant experience. Recognition of significance leads to evaluation. Meanings accompany experience when we know what is happening and what importance the event includes for our personalities. (*Ibid.*, p. 169)

Knowles credits Lindeman with having identified key assumptions about adult learners that have been supported by later research and that constitute the foundation stones of modern adult learning theory:

1. Adults are motivated to learn as they experience needs and interests that learning will satisfy; therefore, these are the appropriate starting points for organizing adult learning activities.

2. Adults' orientation to learning is life-centered; therefore, the appropriate units for organizing adult learning are life situations, not subjects.

3. Experience is the richest resource for adults' learning; therefore, the core methodology of adult education is the analysis of experience.

4. Adults have a deep need to be self-directing; therefore, the role of the teacher is to engage in a process of mutual inquiry with them rather than to transmit his or her knowledge to them and then evaluate their conformity of it.

5. Individual differences among people increase with age; therefore, adult education must make optimal provision for differences in style, time, place, and pace of learning. (1978, p. 31)

Carl Rogers, the humanist psychologist further developed the importance of experience in learning, as he defined two kinds of learning. One kind of learning is cognitive learning that does not involve feelings or personal meanings or relevance for the whole person. The second kind of learning is that which is significant, meaningful, and experiential (1983).

The elements of this second experiential learning are:

- it has a quality of personal involvement (both feeling and cognitive aspects are involved in the learning)

- it is self-initiated (the sense of discovery comes from within the person)

- it is pervasive (it makes a difference in the behavior, the attitudes, perhaps even the personality of the learner)

- it is evaluated by the learner (she knows whether it is meeting her need, whether it leads to what she wants to know or whether it illuminates the dark area of ignorance she is experiencing)

- its essence is meaning (the element of meaning to the learner is built into the whole experience). (p. 20)

Rogers brought a humanist perspective and integration of psychotherapy concepts to the concept of learning for adults. He hypothesized that a person learns significantly only those things that he perceives as being involved in the maintenance of, or enhancement of, the structure of self. If one is truly to become a fully functioning person, then learning is a critical component of the person's development (1961).

Cyril Houle (1961) in his work at the University of Chicago identified the nature of why and how adults learn. In his study of adult learners, he developed a typology based on the purposes of the learning activities. The first type is the goal-oriented learner, who uses education for accomplishing clear-cut objectives. The second type are activity-oriented learners who take part in learning activities as part of social contact and their need for activity. The third type of learner are those who are learning-oriented, who seek knowledge for its own sake. Houle further identified that these learning-oriented learners had engaged in learning without support or assistance; they were self-directed.

This work was followed closely by Allan Tough (1967), who described adult self-teaching and learning projects in his doctoral dissertation. He laid the cornerstone for subsequent research on learning by defining "learning projects," a series of "related episodes, adding up to at least seven hours." (1979, p.7). This was a deliberate learning process, an intended change. He explored the motivation for starting learning projects and found that his subjects had anticipated outcomes and benefits for their learning. The outcomes expected were varied: to satisfy curiosity; to enjoy the content of learning itself; to practice their skills; to impart knowledge or skills to others; to attain understanding of a situation.

Malcolm Knowles contributed to the field of adult learning by utilizing the term "andragogy" to define the unique ways in which adults learn and to provide a theoretical construct to the phenomenon (1972). He outlined assumptions of andragogy to include: changes in adult self-concept, the role of experience, readiness to learn, and orientation to learning. Changes in adult self-concept assumes that as a person grows and matures, his self-concept moves from total dependency (as in an infant) to one of increasing self-directedness. When one assumes self-direction, the person becomes an adult psychologically. The role of experience assumes that as an individual matures, he accumulates an expanding reservoir of experience that causes him to become a rich resource for learning, and provides a basis to which to relate new learnings. Readiness to learn assumes that as an individual matures, her readiness to learn is decreasingly the product of her biological development and academic preparation. The importance of this assumption lies in the importance of timing learning experiences to coincide with the learners' developmental tasks. The assumptions behind orientation to learning related to how adults are problem-oriented, that is, they come into an educational activity largely because they are experiencing some inadequacy or lack of knowledge in dealing with a real life problem. The adult wants to apply tomorrow what she learns today, so time perspective is critical due to the desire to apply the learning immediately.

Knowles further refines his approach to adult learning by providing definition to the concept of self-directed learning as "a process in which individuals take the initiative, with or without the help of others, in diagnosing their learning needs, formulating learning goals, identifying human and material resources for learning, choosing and implementing appropriate learning strategies and evaluating learning outcomes." (1975, p.8). He further made five assumptions about self-directed learning: that the human being grows in capacity and, since self-direction is necessary for maturation, it should be nurtured to develop; learners' experiences are a rich resource for learning; individuals become ready to learn what is required to perform their evolving life task or cope with life problems and everyone has different patterns of readiness; learning experiences should be task-accomplishing or problem solving; and learners are motivated by the need for esteem, the desire to achieve, the urge to grow, the satisfaction of accomplishment, the need to know something specific, and curiosity.

Tough (1967) and Knowles (1975) both described learning as a self-directed and linear prócess. The learner decides what he/she wants to study, then formulates goals, and then proceeds to select learning activities, resources, and ways to evaluate the learning. Evidence now suggests that the self-directed adult learner rarely plans and uses numerous paths to acquire the knowledge he or she seeks (Merriam and Caffarella, 1991). Self-directed learning is not age-related, learning experiences are largely problem-centered, and experience is integral to learning (Ellsworth, 1992).

Spear and Mocker (1984) identified the "Organizing Circumstance," which proposes that self-directed learners, rather than pre-planning their learning projects, tend to select a course from limited alternatives which occur conveniently within their environment (1984). They identified four categories of environmental structuring of learning: the impetus for the learning project is sparked by a change in life circumstances; the now changed circumstances provide limited opportunities for learning; resources for learning are nonetheless found in the circumstances; and learning sequences build on each other in a sequential fashion. The concept that self-directed learners look to their immediate environment for assistance is corroborated by Penland's (1979) survey findings that self-directed learners identified friends or relatives who are experts, books, close friends, and travel as important resources for their learning.

The role of environment in the process of self-directed learning has been expanded by Spear (1988) to include clusters of knowledge and action. The Knowledge cluster is composed of two types of knowledge which the learner brings to the learning: residual knowledge (prior learnings) and acquired knowledge (new knowledge learned as a result of the learning project). The Action cluster is composed of directed action (toward a known or specific end), exploratory (action chosen by the learner without knowing what the outcomes will be) and fortuitous action (action that the learner takes for reasons not related to the learning project). Consistent environment (human and material elements that are regularly in place and generally accessible) and fortuitous environment (chance encounters that aren't expected or foreseen, yet affect the learner and the project) are the two clusters of Environment. Learning projects are gathered around these clusters and may or may not be organized in a linear path; when organization of the clusters occurs and the learner decides what is most/least important the learner is in the greatest control.

Internalization of the learning content is an important dimension in the discussion of self-directed learning. Brookfield reiterated the personal development dimension of adulthood when he described self-directed learning as:

> the mode of learning characteristic of an adult who is in the process of realizing his or her adulthood is concerned as much with an internal change of consciousness as with the external management of instructional events. The most complete form of self-directed learning occurs when process and reflection are married in the adult's pursuit of meaning. (1985, p. 58)

This definition suggests a deeper internalization of the knowledge gained in the self-directed learning process than the mere acquisition of knowledge. Internal change of consciousness is accomplished through critical reflection, is essential to adults, and is an integral part of learning (Mezirow, 1985, Brookfield, 1985, Garrison, 1987). Critical reflection is not just concerned with the how or how-to of action but with the why, the reasons for and consequences of what we do. Critical reflection always involves learning as a process of making a new or revised interpretation of the meaning of experience. (Mezirow, 1985). Learning occurs when information is processed cognitively through critical reflection, and the individual decides to make changes in their behavior (Bandura, 1977, Argyris and Schon, 1974). These concepts have their antecedents in Rogerian humanistic philosophy (1961, 1969). Learning can yield meaningful transformations in individuals (Candy, 1991).

To add further definition to self-directed learning, Candy (1991) defines self-directed learning as four phenomena: "self-direction" as a personal attribute (personal autonomy), "self-direction" as the willingness and capacity to conduct one's own education, "self-direction" as a mode of organizing instruction in formal settings, and "self-direction" as the individual, noninstitutional pursuit of learning opportunities in natural settings (autodidaxy).

Autonomy of the learner is a vital component of the discussion on self-directed learning. Chene (1983) defines autonomy as independence and the will to learn, stating that learners must have an awareness of the learning process, have an understanding of what is conceived as competence in a study area, have the ability to make critical judgments, and be the agents of their own learning. Candy (1991) proposes that autonomous behavior is situational, dependent on the context of the learning. Adults vary in their desire, capacity, and readiness to exert control over their learning (Pratt, 1988).

Long (1989) also supports an individualized approach to self-directed learning in his belief that there are three elements to self-directed learning: the social level (referring to the isolation of the learner), the pedagogical level (where the learner has to identify his/her learning needs, organize a strategy, and gain the resources), and the psychological level (the mental activity of the learner). The psychological component is the most critical element to determining self-directed learning; the learning can occur only when the learners control their learning processes. Psychological control is necessary and sufficient for an activity to be described self-directed.

Brockett and Hiemstra (1991) holistically unite the varying concepts of self-directed learning in their Personal Responsibility Orientation, grounded in what they call "self-direction in learning." They identify two dimensions: self-directed learning (those instructional processes whereby learners assume primary responsibility for planning, implementing, and evaluating their learning) and learner self-direction (which centers on a learner's desire or preference for assuming responsibility for learning). "Self-directed learning" refers to the instructional method while "learner self-direction" relates to the personality characteristics that would lead to the learning method used.

Another dimension of importance to the self-directed learning process is the ability of the learner to learn. The whole issue of "learning to learn" is explored by Smith (1991) who takes Kolb's lead in recognizing that "continuous, lifelong learning requires learning how to learn and this involves appreciation of and competence in diverse approaches to creating, manipulating, and communicating knowledge." The ability to exert control over one's learning demands an attitudinal disposition and a self-concept of potency and self-efficacy, in addition to certain technical learning skills (Candy in Smith, 1991).

Studies have examined and verified self-directed learning for various occupational groups: among them, nurses (Kathrein, 1981, Oddi, Ellis, Roberson, 1990), engineers (Rymell, 1981) farmers (Bayha, 1984), in older adults (Hiemstra, 1976, Sears, 1989), in black adults (Shackelford, 1983), in prospective parents (Cobb, 1978), in clergy (Morris, 1978), and in adult basic education students (Kratz, 1978) and graduate students (Adenuga, 1989). There have not been any studies examining female entrepreneurs and their use of self-directed learning. Self-directed learning has been identified as a common learning strategy by top-level managers who took the initiative in finding out what they needed to know; they were the "ultimate architects of their own development" (Dechant, 1992).

Another approach to the development of management skills is a study conducted by Van Velsor and Hughes (1990), examining how women managers learn. Through content analysis of interviews conducted with seventy-eight women, they found that the learning of women was focused on discovering who they were as individuals in their organizations, on finding their niche, and on integrating self with their environment. Opportunities for learning came from assignments (including first supervisory jobs), from other people, and from hardships. Significant findings of this study were that over fifty percent of the women reported learning from other people and that reflective learnings about self and about self in relation to others were ranked in the top third of all experiences which the women reported.

Lombardo (1982) studied managerial learning without regard to gender differences. His studies reinforce a self-fulfilling prophecy approach where success in management breeds more success. Potential leaders cited having opportunities to experience significant learnings in their careers: learning to delegate, learning how to get advice, setting life goals, discovering strengths, dealing with adversity, and struggling with change.

FEMINIST RESEARCH AND THE USE OF QUALITATIVE METHODS

In the last twenty years, it has been recognized that research in the social sciences has been primarily the research of man, often generalized to include or exclude women (Gilligan, 1983, Jayaratyne and Stewart, 1991, Morgan, 1981). A corollary to this recognition is a criticism that traditional quantitative methodologies are imbued with masculine values and beliefs and, hence, do not adequately explore the phenomenon of women's lives. Specifically, this criticism is rooted in at least three sources: first, negative personal experiences with traditional research; second, a belief that quantitative methodologies support sexist, racist, and elitist attitudes and practices and therefore, negatively affect people's lives; and third, a general rejection of positivism and its claim that science is value neutral (Jayaratyne and Stewart, 1991).

The feminist perspective, then, as presented in feminist research, is used as a lens through which to view the process of inquiry and its social, historical, and political context (Fonow and Cook, 1991). Feminist scholarship supports consciousness raising (ending oppression of disadvantaged groups), incorporation of action in the research, attention to the affective domain (the emotional response in inquiry), and concern with the everyday life world. Feminist practices value connectiveness, cooperation, and mutuality over separativeness, competition, and individual success and aims to produce conditions that benefit women (Martin, 1992).

It has been proposed that quantitative methods can be used in feminist research despite their roots in sexist and antifeminist attitudes; however, quantitative methods may never provide the "richly textured 'feeling for the data' that qualitative methods can permit' (*Ibid.*, p. 93).

Ward (1985) identified four common overlapping deficiencies in traditional quantitative research methodologies: omission and underrepresentation of women as research subjects, concentration on masculine dominated sectors of social life, use of paradigms, concepts, methods, and theories that more closely represented men's rather than women's experiences, and the use of men and their lifestyles as the norms against which social phenomena were interpreted. In gathering information from the male perspective, meaning of the experience is presented through what may be a totally different reality. What is obtained is "a colonized meaning perspective," an unauthentic set of assumptions that usurp the experiential concepts that women develop (Hart, 1990). If the research does not include women in the samples, we cannot automatically transfer the conclusions as true for women. It is, therefore, important that women researchers continue to study the feminist experience in order to provide meaning and understanding of reality for women.

One of the philosophical foundations of feminist research is based on the premise that women define self in terms of connections and relationships, while the male voice defines self in terms of distinctness and separation from others (Gilligan, 1982).

> From the different dynamics of separation and attachment in their gender identity formation through the divergence of identity and intimacy that marks their experience in the adolescent years, male and female voices typically speak of the importance of different truths, the former of the role of separation as it defines and empowers the self, the latter of the ongoing process of attachment that creates and sustains the human community. (p. 156)

Gilligan refers to the moral development of women which, different than the development of men, inculcates an ethic of caring and responsibility.

> As we have listened for centuries to the voices of men and the theories of development that their experience informs, so we have come more recently to notice not only the silence of women but the difficulty in hearing what they say when they speak. Yet in the different voice of women lies the truth of an ethic of care, the tie between relationship and responsibility, and the origins of aggression in the failure of connection. (p. 173)

Further, Gilligan believes that the failure to see the different reality of women's lives stems in part from the assumption that there is a single mode of social experience and interpretation. A more complex rendition of human experience, a more generative view of human life, is possible if the truth of separation and attachment in the lives of women and men are recognized to have different meanings for both.

Reinforcing the theme of women's linkages with others, we find that concepts of women's development differ from those of Levinson and Erikson, who primarily focused on male development. Merriam and Clark (1991) have acknowledged that interrelatedness, connectedness, and caring are the "lens" through which women interpret the world, while work is important for identity and self-definition (p. 15). A woman's web of relationships (primary family, husband, partners, children, and friends) is central to her development (Josselson, 1987). The development of feminine personality is defined in early socialization in relation and connection to other people (Chodorow, 1974). She suggests that this has developed through nurturing and socializer roles of women. Miller suggests that the organizing principle for women's lives is doing for others, hence, women tend to put the needs of others first (1986).

A new model of feminine development illustrates the critical factors affecting a woman's self-knowledge during her adult years. The process of development is viewed as a spiraling funnel, influenced by the moment in time and her sphere of influence and relationships (family, friends, and work). A woman's ability to both influence and change her web of relationships allows her to expand her definition of self (Peck, 1986).

Building on the foundation established by Gilligan, Belenky, Clinchy, Goldberger, and Tarule (1986) conducted an extensive research project that examined "women's ways of knowing." They explored and describe five perspectives (types) from which women view reality and draw conclusions about truth, knowledge, and authority. Their study has particular relevance to this research study for its study of women and learning using an qualitative approach: The researchers conducted interviews with 135 "ordinary women with ordinary lives" (p. 4) to "hear what was important about life and learning" from the woman interviewee's point of view (p. 11).

Five epistemological categories were identified: silence (women experiencing themselves as mindless, voiceless, and subordinate to external authority); received knowledge (women conceiving themselves as receiving knowledge from all-knowing external authorities, not capable of creating knowledge on their own); subjective knowledge (where truth and knowledge are conceived of as personal, private and intuitive); procedural knowledge (women investing in learning and applying objective procedures for obtaining and communicating knowledge); and constructed knowledge (women viewing all knowledge as contextual, creating knowledge, and valuing both subjective and objective strategies for knowing).

In Silence, the woman is seen but never heard. There is an absence of the voice. This position represents an extreme in self-denial and blind obedience to external authority for direction. Women in this stage of knowing wait to be told by others, without rationale or reason. They are selfless and voiceless. Belenky, et al, maintain that anyone emerging from their childhood years as the women in this stage signals "the failure of the community to receive all of those entrusted in its care" (p. 34). In Received Knowledge, the woman learns by listening. The ideas that are heard are in the words of others and they are concrete and dualistic, that is, right or wrong, black or white, true or false. Received knowers are very open to take in what others have to offer, but they have little confidence in their own ability to speak. They believe that all knowledge originates outside of themselves and they look to others for self-knowledge.

In Subjective Knowledge, Belenky, et al, identify two stages: the inner voice and the quest for self. In Subject Knowing, truth resides within the person and can negate answers that the world supplies. The inner voice is a new experience. In discovering her inner voice, it becomes a source of strength to the woman. There is a growing reliance on intuitive processes. The subjectivist finds that each person's life experience gives a different view of reality from that of any other person. Truth is a private matter and should not be imposed on others. Subjectivist women distrust logic, analysis, abstraction, and even language itself. They resent any authority figures. Often the subjectivist, as she acts on her new conceptions of truth, takes new steps in her life by making a break with her past and former relationships, hence the quest for self. The primary learning mode is of inward listening and watching. The subjectivist knower is stubbornly immune to other people's ideas (p. 98).

In Procedural Knowledge, the way of knowing is through conscious, deliberate, and systematic analysis. Form is more important than content: the procedural knower acquires and applies procedures for obtaining and communicating knowledge. They pay attention to objects in the external world. Here again, there are two emergent patterns: one is the separate knowing and connected knowing. Separate knowers' procedures for making meaning are impersonal; feelings and personal beliefs are excluded. In this mode, the knower's own concerns are ignored and adopting a neutral, non-offensive perspective. She doesn't want to be blinded by her emotions or opinions. The connected knower believes that most trustworthy knowledge comes from personal experience rather than from authorities. She develops procedures to gather information from the authority/expert. She uses empathy to focus on the ways others think, never arguing but accepting.

The Constructed Knowledge way of knowing integrates the voices. Constructivists identify their selves by integrating knowledge that they believe is intuitively personally important with knowledge they have learned from others. "They develop a narrative sense of the self--past and future" (p. 136). Constructivists express an interest in their personal history and use critical self-reflection. Life is not an "either/or" for these women; they allow for the richness of the varied roles of their lives and do not limit themselves because a role may produce stress or conflict. They appreciate the complexity of their situation. For this group, "all knowledge is constructed, and the knower is an intimate part of the known (p. 137)." Constructivists engage in lifelong learning, searching for the truth, and a passion for knowing.

For the constructivist, posing questions is central to the way she knows. Constructivists also have a strong sense of responsibility, of "caring for people," and they strive to demonstrate a conviction for taking action to do something for their community. Constructivist women seek balance in their lives; they honor the needs of others as well as their own; and they desire quality of life for themselves and others.

The aforementioned research studies are representative of the approach advocated by Acker, Barry and Esseveld (1991): a radical rebeginning in feminist research in which what is to be explained is what actually happens in women's everyday world and how these events are experienced. This is a method of exploration and discovery, one of using an open and critical process where all previously held assumptions within the social sciences are reexamined for relevancy and appropriateness. One such assumption is that the researcher must be a neutral observer. This assumption is challenged by those who feel that the researcher be aware that their personal response to the object of research leads to a bias in the analysis and interpretation of research data. Both Oakley (1981) and Kirkwood (1993) maintain that the emotional involvement of the researcher helps understand the reality of the object being studied: having personal knowledge and empathy helps formulate a more concise phenomenological interpretation. Hence, the researcher cannot remain aloof or detached in the interview process (Oakley, 1981, Mishler, 1986); by the very nature of feminist research, the personal dimension minimizes the traditional "interviewer-interviewee" relationship in favor of a nonhierarchical, equalized discourse model. Optimally, the feminist researcher is prepared to invest her own personal identity in the relationship.

ENTREPRENEURSHIP AND WOMAN ENTREPRENEURS

A dramatic increase in the amount of entrepreneurial "start-ups" and entrepreneurial activity occurred in the 1980's, resulting in a renewed research interest on the part of academics to explore this phenomenon (Solomon and Winslow, 1988). The literature presents diverse definitions of an entrepreneur:

> "independently owned and operated business with less than 100 employees or less than $1,000,000 gross receipts per year." (Bart, 1983)

> "the process of creating something different with value by devoting the necessary time and effort; assuming the accompanying financial, psychic, and social risks; and receiving the resulting rewards of monetary and personal satisfaction." (Bowen and Hisrich, 1986)

> "one who takes an active role in the decision making and risk taking of a business in which s/he has majority ownership." (U.S. Department of Commerce, 1986)

> "voluntary initiator of change, constantly on the lookout for new ideas." (Mintzberg, 1990)

"those who develop 'new combinations' that lead to development of new markets, new products, new services, new production and distribution methods." (Schumpeter, 1961)

"one who starts and is successful in a venture and/or project that leads to profit (monetary or personal) or benefits society." (Solomon and Winslow, 1988)

Various studies have explored variables essential for success as an entrepreneur. Qualities for entrepreneurial success have been identified as ambition, high self-esteem, energy, competitiveness, achievement motivation, willingness to assume risk, and a high need for independence (Schwartz, 1976). In a study of seventy-four small firms, Ibrahim and Goodwin (1987) found that entrepreneurial behavior (demonstrated by personality attributes such as intuition, extroversion, taking risks, creativity, flexibility, sense of independence, and having a value for time) and management skills (cash flow management, niche strategy, pre-ownership experience, education, delegation, knowledge of organizational structure) are the two critical dimensions for success.

A study of successful entrepreneurs conducted under the auspices of the international consulting firm, McBer and Company, identified three important characteristics. They seem more proactive (do things before they have to and don't let things slide). They show characteristics associated with achievement motivation syndrome: they seize unusual opportunities, they take moderate risks, they are concerned about doing things better and about high quality of work, they define sub-goals and means of reaching them, and they monitor by holding people to high standards of work quality. The third group of competencies involves commitment to others, especially as it relates to customer satisfaction (McClelland, 1987). The McBer study further did not identify any significant correlation between business success and any of the following variables: number of previous jobs held, highest level of education, father's occupation or mother's occupation. The findings strongly suggest that it is not a person's position in life, or the initial advantage they have that contributes to their success in business but, rather certain personality characteristics or competencies.

W. Gibb Dyer, Jr., in his research with entrepreneurs at Brigham Young University, also identified nine characteristics essential for entrepreneurial success: the ability to take risks, the desire to compete, the ability to handle stress, the ability to make work fun, the ability to creatively solve problems, the ability to recognize opportunities, the commitment to the business, goal orientation, and realistic optimism (1992). Dyer has also found that themes of working hard, self-reliance, a determination to succeed, and a knack for finding and developing opportunities as learned through early childhood experiences is characteristic of the entrepreneurs he has studied.

Winslow and Solomon have postulated that entrepreneurs are slightly sociopathic in that their perception of self is that they are slightly "different" in comparison with the general population (1989). Among the behaviors which describe this "sociopathic" description include having a concept of the future guided by one's own sense of fantasy of the future and the ability to influence, achievement motivated in the sense of using their own ability to influence outcomes and providing constant attention to environment, possible opportunities and misfortunes.

Much of the research on entrepreneurs has focused on the experiences of male entrepreneurs and has focused on background factors and personal characteristics, psychological attributes and traits, and situational factors (Stevenson, 1990, Bowen and Hisrich, 1986, McClelland, 1961, 1986, Welsh and White, 1983, Baumol, 1983, Solomon and Winslow, 1988, 1989).

The most prevalent reason for the exclusion of women in these early research studies is two-fold. The numbers of female entrepreneurs were initially small. Most women-owned businesses have not been in existence for more than twenty years. Between 1972 and 1982, the number of female-owned businesses increased by 69 per cent (Scott, 1986). Underrepresentation in the population may have accounted for underrepresentation in the literature.

A second suggested reason for the exclusion of women is male-bias toward women in entrepreneurial research (Stevenson, 1990, Moore, 1990). Specific actions to exclude women from research studies (Hornaday and Aboud, 1971, McClelland, 1961) reflect the bias that was further demonstrated by Collins and Moore (1970), who suggested that entrepreneurship was a way of demonstrating maleness (Wilkins, 1979). Many of the businesses owned by women are in the personal service and retailing industries; perhaps these are perceived as not having the same research value significance as technical organizations, which tend to be led by males (Bowen and Hisrich, 1986).

Attempts to develop a "profile" of the average *female entrepreneur* have yielded disparate images. The female entrepreneur is an individual who Hisrich and Bowen (1986) describe by a general set of characteristics:

- the first born

- from a middle or upper class family

- the daughter of a self-employed parent

- educated to degree level

- married with children

- age of forty to forty-five at start up

- unlikely to start a business in traditionally male-dominated industries

- possess relevant experience

- experiencing a need for additional managerial training.

Reasons for women to start their own businesses are to be one's own boss, to have a challenge, and to have the opportunity to make more money (Scott, 1986). Subsequent research identified similarities in the start-up motivations of male and female entrepreneurs: both cited need for money, wish to be independent, and identification of business opportunities. (Goffee and Scase 1985, Birley, 1989, Cromie, 1987).

Another common reason for women to start their business is as accommodation to the demands on their personal lives, i.e., as primary caretakers for their small children (Scott, 1986). Despite the benefits of running one's own business and having greater flexibility, they experience more pressure to manage family with work than most men (Stevenson, 1986, Neider, 1987, Longstreth and associates, 1987, Stoner, Hartman, and Arora, 1990, Simpson, 1991).

Women entrepreneurs are characterized as being highly motivated with a high degree of internal locus of control and achievement orientation (Bowen and Hisrich 1986, Neider 1987, Waddell 1983, Bernay, 1988). They have high needs for self-fulfillment, desire to achieve, and interests in helping others (1989 Avon Report). They have demonstrated high levels of endurance (persistence), dominance (need to influence others to do what one wants), achievement, intraception (need to analyze the motives of others and predict behavior accordingly), and autonomy (Neider, 1987, Schwartz, 1976).

At the start of their businesses, female entrepreneurs tend to use an autocratic approach (Schwartz, 1976). As the organization stabilizes, they may be comfortable using participatory styles of leadership which demonstrate a high degree for people (Chaganti, 1986) and are especially inclined to do so if their businesses are small. Research further indicates that as organizational leaders, women entrepreneurs tend toward micro-managing their employees and are reluctant to delegate (Neider, 1987, Cuba, DeCenzo, and Anish, 1983, Schwartz, 1976). Two major strengths identified for female entrepreneurs were high energy levels and skill in influencing others (Neider, 1987).

Educationally, female entrepreneurs have been found to be more highly educated than their male counterparts and the general population (Stevenson, 1986, Longstreth, Stafford, and Maudlin, 1987, Cuba, DeCenzo and Anish, 1983) although they often have a degree in liberal arts and not in business (Stevenson, 1986, Hisrich and Brush, 1983, Scott, 1986).

The need for training in business management and strategy has been identified for female entrepreneurs (Bart, 1983, Diffley, 1983). Chaganti found that management skills were developed through self-enrollment in courses in financial management and business planning (1986). These women reported using external sources of management and technical expertise, such as government agencies and business associations apparently recognized their weaknesses and took steps to fill the gaps.

Nelson examined the information needs of one hundred female entrepreneurs and found that networks and significant others ("a current close personal associate, familial or not, whose opinion of such value that it would be specifically sought and could cause one to change a decision") had a strong influence on female entrepreneurs (1987). Nelson has further studied the role of the "significant other" and determined that spouses, siblings, and male friends made the most meaningful contributions to women entrepreneurs, based on their ability to make a meaningful contribution (1989). The Florida female entrepreneurs researched extensively by Neider (1987) used male mentors and personal business advisors. Women entrepreneurs have indicated a need to acquire information on preparing budgets, taxes, business plans, record-keeping and legal requirements (Nelson, 1987, Scott, 1986). Identification of resources for business training is a difficulty for all entrepreneurs (Schwartz, 1976). Women do engage in reading trade magazines and this form of self-learning was positively related to sales and profit (Cuba, DeCenzo and Anish, 1983).

It has been suggested that business schools take a role in developing entrepreneurial behavior and managerial skills through entrepreneurship education (Ibrahim and Goodwin, 1987, Zeithaml and Rice, 1987). It has been found that university small business programs, past college courses, and the chamber of commerce were rated the lowest in usefulness, usage, and cost as sources of information for female entrepreneurs (Nelson, 1987).

WOMEN AND LEADERSHIP

In the field of leadership studies, the same pattern of underrepresentation in the literature prevails as demonstrated in the area of entrepreneurs. Up until the 1970's, much of the research on leadership has dealt almost exclusively with male subjects, reflecting the reality that very few women occupied leadership positions (Kovalainen, 1988, Gale, 1989). However, there is evidence that a bias against women existed here as well, for women were not widely viewed as possessing leadership ability (Bass, Grussell, & Alexander, 1971, Schein, 1973, Hollander and Yoder, 1984, Krebs, 1988, Kanter, 1977). Gale suggests that a basic organizing concept of our culture is that women are subordinate to men, thus leadership historically has been considered a male domain (1989).

The concept of leader was more closely associated with the task orientation of men (Anderson and McLenigan, 1987) and leader positions have been described in terms of the "male managerial model" (Russell, Rush and Herd, 1988). Culturally and socially determined gender differentiation as well as role expectations often kept women from actively pursuing leadership positions (Megargee, 1975, Stevenson, 1990, Longstreth, Stafford, Maudlin, 1987, Scherer, Brodzinski, and Wiebe, 1990, Riding and Swift, 1990, Birley,1989, Denmark, 1977).

Baraka-Love (1986) identified variables that have contributed to the growth and development of successful women who have reached leadership positions in their fields. She found that successful women have supportive family backgrounds (regardless of race of socioeconomic status), high achievement during their school years, positive role models, an awareness of inequities in organizations, and an ability to confront and to overcome negative social forces directed towards women. Another study of well-educated women business leaders (women who own businesses of annual sales volume of $5 million or run a corporate division of $20 million of sales) compiled a database of their family and educational backgrounds, major life events, and the relationship of competency and success. The results of the study suggested that female competency is enhanced by work experience, and that past and present supportive relationships with parents and spouses play an important role towards the development of feelings of competency (Goldwasser, 1988).

The importance of relationships in developing leaders is further demonstrated in the influence of role models (Haas, 1992). Leaders can learn by watching and following role models, a means of gaining knowledge and social understanding. Women in management may be reluctant to accept the role of role model because it places additional pressures on them. However, women managers in top leadership positions assist other women while they are looking out for themselves, recognizing that their own success in organizations is fragile (Morrison, White, Van Velsor, and the Center for Creative Leadership, 1992).

The bias against women as leaders often blocked women in their attempts to climb corporate ladders to executive levels. Many women employees of established companies or corporations discovered a "Glass Ceiling" above which they could not be promoted, an invisible barrier prohibiting entry to the senior management ranks primarily inhabited by white males (Morrison, White, Van Velsor, and others, 1987, Scase, Goffee, and Mann, 1987, Chaganti, 1986, Master, 1989). Upon reaching this "Glass Ceiling," these women often resigned and started up their own businesses, hence business ownership became one method of circumventing a male-dominated system and satisfying one's career goals.

Recent studies of how women lead indicate that women tend to use more socially facilitative behaviors to lead, while men use a more task-focused style (Eagly and Karau, 1991, Helgesen, 1990). This "interactive" style of leading, using a cooperative, people-centered approach as opposed to a "transactional" approach based on dominance, is becoming more acceptable as the importance of social relationships in organizations becomes increasingly evident (Rosener 1990, Peters and Waterman, 1982, Astin and Leland, 1991). Both Rosener (1990) and Peters (1990) suggest that women's styles of leadership should be the norm to which men are compared.

These findings were also supported in a study of leadership behaviors of community college presidents (Roueche, Baker, Rose, 1989). Although the high-achieving women in the study exhibited strong characteristics in all dimensions of leadership (vision, influence, people, values, and motivation) which matched closely the men's scores, there were differences in areas where the women displayed stronger behaviors than the men and vice-versa. Women demonstrated stronger behaviors in vision (taking appropriate risks to bring about change), in influence (able to cause followers to solve problems to work together), in people (demonstrating respect and care for individual differences), and in values (building openness and trust through personal and professional behavior).

Riane Eisler refers to the differences in styles used by males and females as "dominator" or "partner" models based on larger societal constructs, with the female leaders using generally more egalitarian social structures (in Barrentine,1993).

Helgesen (1990) utilized an interview technique similar to that used by Henry Mintzberg to compare the leadership tasks of women and men. She found that women had certain advantages in their ability to communicate, to prioritize, to see the broad picture, based on the changing requirements of today's organizations. Today's reinvented organizations are "ecological, stressing the interrelatedness of all things" (p. 30), values which are shared by the women in Helgesen's study.

QUALITATIVE RESEARCH AND FEMALE ENTREPRENEUR RESEARCH

Qualitative research methodology has been supported in the literature as the most appropriate way to explore women's studies. It has been postulated that the quantitative methods that look into "research objects" which have been detached from their real-life surroundings are less useful to women's research than qualitative methods which do not break living connections (Mies, 1991).

The need to research women entrepreneurs as a group distinct from their male counterparts has been identified (Stevenson, 1990) in order to establish a profile that is consistent with the experiences of women, not necessarily the same as those of men. The qualitative research model has been used in numerous research studies on entrepreneurs (Solomon and Winslow, 1988) and has support as a method to acquire rich information about the world of female entrepreneurs (Stevenson, 1990).

The qualitative approach contrasts sharply with the paradigm of experimental design, positivism, and quantitative research methods. Key concepts associated with the qualitative approach are: definition of a situation, common sense understanding and meaning of a phenomenon, and use of description and soft data (Bogden and Biklen, 1982). Quantitative methods are concerned with replication of the phenomenon, hypothesis testing through control of variables in research and the use of statistics and hard data (Kerlinger, 1986).

In naturalistic qualitative inquiry, there is no statistical measurement to corroborate or negate a hypothesis. The researcher does not enter the investigation with a set of theories to prove or disprove: the main criteria is an open mind that can accept emerging facets of a problem which may not have existed in the researcher's worldview (Marsick, 1990). The validity and dependency on the human being as an instrument is paramount for creating a theory, for generalizing a "truth." The human perceptions, beliefs, viewpoints are the measure of validity.

SUMMARY

The research indicates that learning is on going, natural, and a vital part of adult life. Adult learning is characterized by its reliance on experience of the adult learner. A process of adult learning, self-directed learning, is characterized by individual autonomy, personal responsibility, initiative and independence, a future orientation, and the ability to control one's endeavors. These characteristics have also been used to describe the woman entrepreneur.

Most entrepreneurial research has been conducted on males. A profile of female entrepreneurs is suggested in the research. There are a variety of reasons for engaging in entrepreneurial behavior and female entrepreneurs have been studied to examine their differences with men and success factors.

Qualitative approaches to research have been identified in the literature as suitable and desirable for research in the areas of learning, entrepreneurial studies, and women's studies. Feminist literature supports the use of in-depth interviews and utilization of women's experiences for interpretation. Further, the research suggests that women's voices must be heard as an important part of theory building. Interconnectedness and relationships with others is another important dimension of the development of women.

Studies on the ways that women lead have demonstrated that women tend to use a more relationship-oriented, participative style of leadership which is a more people-oriented approach. It has been suggested that women's ways of leading are more effective in the new collaborative organization. Chapter Three will discuss the naturalistic qualitative research approach as it applies to the design of this study.

III
Methodology of the Study

INTRODUCTION

Since learning has been acknowledged as a natural phenomenon of adult life (Tough 1979, Knox 1977, Knowles 1975), it was appropriate to use a research approach that investigated and described the phenomenon in its natural state. The naturalistic paradigm, or set of assumptions, were selected for this research study given the nature of the research question, that is, explore the phenomenon of learning in the life of female entrepreneurs. This paradigm consists of a set of assumptions for viewing the social world.

The naturalistic approach was selected for this study as opposed to a positivistic approach for a variety of reasons. In naturalistic qualitative inquiry, there is no statistical measurement to corroborate or negate a hypothesis. The researcher does not enter the investigation with a set of theories to prove or disprove: the main criteria is an open mind that can accept emerging facets of a problem which may not have existed in the researcher's worldview (Marsick, 1990). Qualitative researchers study qualities or entities and seek to understand them in a particular context. Qualitative looks at the "what," whereas quantitative looks at the "how much" (Smith, 1987).

Qualitative research supports the validity and dependency on the human being as an instrument is paramount for creating a theory, for generalizing a "truth." Human perception, feeling, and experience is the scientific instrumentation chosen for studying human life (Spindler, 1970). These are reported in the qualitative study through narrative vignettes, quotations from observational field notes and interviews, and the use of ethnographic tools such as life history and remembering (Smith, 1987). Naturalistic qualitative inquiry is characterized by its holistic examination of a situation (Marsick, 1990). The research is conducted in a natural setting, using the human interviewer as the instrument and building on tacit knowledge (what is already known by interviewee and the interviewer) through the use of qualitative methods. This study used the qualitative methods of purposeful sampling, document review, inclusion of unobtrusive measures, inductive data analysis, grounded theory, and member checks with the respondents prior to the conclusion of the study, following a model established by Lincoln and Guba (1985). It was anticipated that this process would yield a descriptive product that would promote understanding of how the female entrepreneur engages in learning and the shape and substance of learning in her life.

The interactive personal interview was chosen as the primary method of studying the phenomenon of learning for female entrepreneurs. Although the interview has been criticized for its potential difficulties in interviewer bias, inaccuracies, and inconsistencies (Bailey, 1978), it has been lauded as an ideal way to gather data in areas of phenomenological studies, especially in the area of women's studies (Oakley, 1981).

A particular interview technique, The Expressive Autobiographic Interview, developed by Louise Spindler (1970) was used in this study to have the women express in their own words the meaning of learning in their lives. This type of Interview is a cross between a structured interview and a chronological autobiography. It allows the participant to freely contribute in a life story manner. The participants were asked to describe how they had reached their current position as CEO or President of their organization. The question appeared to put the respondents at ease, because they could start wherever they chose and could start with the elements of their lives that they felt were most important. Many started their stories about their childhood. The questioning technique started in this fashion required little prompting for most participants; I only needed to ask questions for clarity and elaboration.

This particular technique allows the interviewed participants to talk about what they consider most important and share information in an emotional atmosphere established by the confidential and uniqueness of their own life story. The participants reveal value orientations, previous experiences, thoughts and perceptions (Spindler, 1970). This technique is very similar to McClelland's Behavioral Event Interview (BEI), in which the interviewee brings up critical events or episodes in life (1986).

Qualitative research methodology has been supported as an appropriate way to investigate the field of women entrepreneurs (Stevenson, 1990, Moore, 1990). This methodology is also supported as the most appropriate way to research the field of self-directed learning (Brookfield, 1984, Spear & Mocker, 1984, Candy, 1991).

THE SAMPLE: WHO WERE THE PARTICIPANTS?

The interview participant sample for this research consisted of eighteen women selected as typical and convenient cases from a list of women entrepreneurs, the Texas Women's Chamber of Commerce, and their subsequent snowball referrals of those women of other women who meet the criteria for the study. These women operated their businesses in either Austin or San Antonio, Texas.

The criteria for selection for inclusion in this research were that the participant be a women entrepreneur who is President or Chief Executive Officer of an organization that she leads which had not less than ten employees and which had gross annual revenues not less than $1,000,000. These criteria were established to include women in the study who had already overcome the problems associated with startup businesses Businesses which represented by the owners in this sample were:

- a printing and reprographics company

- a franchising headquarters for a merchandise store specializing in back and stress relaxation products undergoing national expansion

- a full-service real estate organization of several companies which included real estate mortgage services, real estate residential sales, and commercial sales

- a temporary placement and personnel placement service

- a semiconductor intermediary process manufacturing organization

- a commercial building contractor

- a road sign and barricade construction company

- a full-service personal services salon

- a specialty ice cream store chain

- an engineering slip ring design and assembly company

- a plumbing service company

- an advertising and public relations firm

- a steel rebar company

- a software development firm that develops tailored programs

- an electronics company

- an office equipment, furniture, and supply company

- a telecommunications equipment company

- a company which creates networks, connecting the right people for partnerships

Four of the women interviewed had been recognized as "Entrepreneur of the Year" in different years by business leaders in Austin and San Antonio for their successful efforts at building healthy, growing businesses. Another had been recognized as a "Who's Who in American Business" and recognized by the Small Business Administration for her leadership and business abilities. I personally knew only one of the women prior to the study as an acquaintance through a professional association. Appendix A provides a short description of the women interviewed in this study.

As the study unfolded and women were identified for inclusion in the sample, demographic characteristics of the women were identified (see Appendix B). Sixteen of the eighteen women were Caucasian non-minority women, while two were of Hispanic origins. Education levels were identified as 1) high school or GED, 2) Bachelor's degree, 3) Advanced degree, and 4) Technical Training. All of the women had completed at least high school or a GED. Age-wise, of the eighteen women interviewed in this study, one was in her early 30's, eleven were in their 40's; five were in their 50's, none were in their 60's, and one was 77 years of age.

PREPARATION OF THE HUMAN INSTRUMENT:
INVESTIGATOR PREPARATION

My preparation as the sole investigator and human instrument for this study began with my analysis of my own skills and experience as an organizational researcher and student of adult learning. I brought certain enhanced skills to the study as a female who had been employed in formal male-dominated organizations and who had started my own business as an organization development consultant and human resource developer. In these capacities, I had designed and developed leadership and supervisory skills development programs, worked on organizational change efforts designed to integrate Total Quality Management into the culture of client organizations, and had been lead consultant on many teambuildings and organizational improvement interventions. Some of my work involved developing the skills needed in teams for self-management. Additionally, I had been a member of several women's networking organizations and had provided voluntary leadership development training and assistance to non-profit groups.

I had spent eighteen years in the field of organizational development prior to the undertaking of the interviews. During that time, I had accumulated much experience listening to organizational members in the interviewer-client arena in the context of organizational diagnosis. This listening involved gathering information, in an investigative mode to determine the actual state of an organization, sometimes determining from interviews a description of the organization much different than that which had been presented by the client who contracted me.

My experiences as an interviewer had taught me the importance of remaining neutral, encouraging, and demonstrating empathy and interest in the commentary of my interviewees. I had learned how to not ask leading questions or prompt for a desired response for I was seeking the "unknown factor," something that perhaps had not been yet uncovered in previous interviews or in my review of organizational records or documents.

In addition to my experience as an organization development consultant prior to the study, I had been a feedback consultant for the Leadership Development Program with the Center for Creative Leadership, TEAM group in San Antonio, Texas. This experience, with senior level executives of varying organizations, involved providing feedback on various diagnosis instruments (FIRO-B, Myers-Briggs Type Indicator, California Psychological Inventory, Kirton Adaptability Inventory, Leadership Skill Inventory, and Shipley IQ) in the context of leadership development training. The feedback interview is an intensive, four-hour long meeting between a participant and the feedback-giver. The instrumentation results are provided to the participant in an interview during which the feedback-giver gently probes into the yet-undivulged background of the participant to determine any links between data presented and data unknown in the history of the interviewee. The feedback-giver has the difficult task of quickly gaining rapport and trust of the participant in order to go over data which is intensely personal and sensitive in a short period of time. Additionally, the interviewer must have good listening skills and integrating skills in order to gather information in the interview that is woven into the overall participant profile. This is crucial if the feedback is to have relevance for the participant and if it is to become the foundation for personal goal setting for personal life changes.

My experience in leadership development programs and work as a coach and consultant to senior leaders and managers at all levels of organizations provided me with a real-time awareness of what effective leaders do in their positions. This would enable me to keep the interviews focused and ask relevant questions of my interviewees.

I also believe that my preparation for the interviews was enhanced by my being a female, my having a family and my having experienced some of the trials and tribulations that women in business often go through. These include managing time demands, family demands, and operating a business. During the summer of 1993, I had the opportunity to attend a summer symposium chaired by Dr. Carolyn Clark at Texas A & M in College Station, Texas, on "The Ways Women Lead." The graduate-level group worked on a qualitative research project: weekly discussions at College Station reviewed interviewing, determining categories for inquiry, and research into the feminist literature on leadership. The seminar series was concluded with a visit from Dr. Rosemary Caffarella of Northern Colorado University and a discussion of her research into the field of feminine leadership.

With this background, I felt prepared to conduct the interviews with the female entrepreneurs identified for the study.

THE INTERVIEW PROTOCOL

Contact was made with the potential interviewees through two primary means: telephone contact and through personal face-to-face contact with subjects at formally organized women's meetings. When using telephone contact, I introduced myself to the participants, indicated if I had been referred to her by another entrepreneur or if I had attained her name from a Business Journal listing, and I asked if the businesswoman would be interested in participating in a research study of female entrepreneurs. The same approach was used when I met a potential interview subject at a public meeting (usually women's meetings). All but two potential interviewees agreed to meet with me. The participants were informed in advance of my intent to tape the interview, as well as to maintain the confidentiality and anonymity of the interview. Although most of the women said they wouldn't mind if I divulged their names, pseudonyms are used in this research report.

Once entry was gained to the interviewee, a suitable schedule and location was arranged to conduct the interview. Some of the women had their secretaries schedule our meetings; most scheduled their own meetings. Potential participants were asked if they could allocate approximately ninety minutes for the interview. Most of the interviews lasted between 45 and 85 minutes. The location of most interviews was at the woman entrepreneur's work place: either an office or a conference room where we were able to meet without interruptions. Seven interviews were conducted in eateries located near to the entrepreneur's work place and were conducted as a lunch or late morning meeting. Two of the meetings were held after the normal workday, three were conducted on a Saturday morning, and the remainder were conducted during the business day.

The interview process was familiar to many of the women. Several had been interviewed and received press coverage locally. In part due to their "notoriety" as local successful entrepreneurs, two of the women were currently engaged in autobiographical projects with other graduate students who were assisting in the writing of their histories. Several of the women had been speakers on panels at the University of Texas Graduate School of Business as well as at local Women's Chamber of Commerce meetings.

The interviewees were reminded of my intent to tape record the conversation in order to ensure that no data be lost or overlooked; each participant agreed to the taping. The women appeared to be comfortable with the taping process: several suggested stopping the tape when the interview was interrupted (i.e. by food delivery or a telephone call) to ensure that the main content would be clear.

Concurrent with the taped record, I took notes to support the interview. Lofland and Lofland (1984) strongly suggest the use of an Interview Guide to assist the researcher with accurate logging of data and provide organization to notetaking. I used an Interview Guide for each interview. The Interview Guide (Appendix C) was a computer-generated form that listed the demographic information about the participant: identification of interviewee, date and place of interview, information regarding age, level of education, race or ethnicity, previous work experience, and family-related information. Also annotated on the form were observations about the woman, her office or business place which could contribute to the profile of the woman by providing background and supporting information.

At the beginning of the interview, I briefly described that this study would be examining various aspects of the life of female entrepreneurs, and that the interview would start off with a general question about how the female entrepreneur got to her current position. I indicated that I would be following up on any items brought up by the woman business owner for clarity or further discussion.

The first question, "How did you get to your current position as the CEO/President of this organization?" allowed the entrepreneur to pick her own starting point. When the interviewee reached a point of satiation with the first question, usually about 35 minutes into the interview, I asked "What do you do in your current role as CEO?" This enabled the interviewee to volunteer the many elements of her role as she saw it and continue to provide information without leading prompts. As the interviewing process progressed, the questioning followed a "focused exploration" approach that allowed for more structure in the interviewing process (Lincoln and Guba, 1986). This allowed me to ask a specific question of the participants in the later interviews on a topic that had been raised during earlier interviews by previous participants. This follows the notion of emergent design: as the interviewing process progresses, data are generated which warrants inclusion in subsequent ongoing interviews.

Prior to the completion of the interview, I conducted a member check with each participant, reviewing and summarizing the data and key points that they had raised during the meeting. This interview method is used to eliminate bias or incorrect interpretation in the field and transcribed notes. It often reminded the participant of a point she had not made earlier and had not taken the opportunity to mention. This process insures that the respondents have an opportunity to assess the information that is being constructed about them, further reinforcing the dimension of trustworthiness of the researcher and the trustworthiness (validity) of the research findings.

Three of the interviewees brought me on a tour of their facilities and introduced me to employees. Employees who were introduced were cordial and polite. One of the women interviewed presented me with a gift of a large bag of pecans from her own pecan trees (so I wouldn't leave empty-handed).

Within a week of the interview, I sent a brief note of appreciation to each of the interviewees, thanking them for their time and contribution of their stories. The tapes were transcribed verbatim, usually within a few days of the interview. and the transcription was reviewed and analyzed.

PILOT STUDY

A small pilot group of interviews was conducted at the start of the project between late June and early August 1993. The purpose of the pilot was to identify any potential problem areas, provided the researcher an opportunity to practice interviewing, and to test the methodology proposed. Six women were contacted and interviewed for the pilot. The interviews generated a significant number of categories from which this researcher could generate subsequent questions for interviewees.

There were several significant learnings that resulted from the review of the pilot. First, I found that I could transcribe the tapes of the meetings held in less-than-ideal taping conditions (i.e. a cafe) because I could remember the context of the conversation and could more accurately transcribe barely audible words easier than someone who had not been there. Second, it became clear that the tapes be transcribed as soon as possible after the interview in order to keep the information fresh and easily remembered. Two tapes, which were transcribed two to three weeks after the interview, were more difficult to transcribe. Third, by listening to the tapes and transcribing myself, I had an opportunity to review any interviewing practices that were less effective than others. In the first set of two or three interviews, I felt that I had spent considerable time in building rapport and occasionally following a conversation trail off the topic along with the woman being interviewed. There is a balance which must be struck in order to assure that the interviewer and interviewee engage in discourse, but not deviate too far from the intention of the interview. Later interviews would provide richer amounts of data for the interviewer became more practiced at keeping the interviewee closer to the topic and focused on the emerging question set.

DATA COLLECTION AND ANALYSIS

The method used in this study allowed that analysis of the data occurred as the interviews progressed. This follows a model presented by Lofland and Lofland (1984, pp. 132) which describes how collection of data relates to analysis over time of the research. Analysis occurs simultaneously to the data collection phase, a necessity for focusing of questions and emerging design of the study.

Once an interview had been conducted, the tapes were transcribed into pages of verbatim text, using computer-assisted word processing software. Each interview was analyzed sentence by sentence for units of analysis. Individual sentences and short paragraphs representing a concise thought were copied to 3 x 5-inch cards. Each card had one unit of analysis, one concise thought. The cards were coded on the back with demographic information pertaining to each woman interviewed. This information included interview sequence number, ethnicity of the interviewee, formal education level, location of the interview, and age of the interviewee.

Once the unitizing process (collecting each thought and copying it to a card) and demographic coding was completed, the interview data were analyzed using an approach that allowed for constant comparison of the interview data to derive a set of "categories" for analysis. The approach suggested by Glaser and Strauss (1967) allowed for the development of deriving theory while processing data. This was further operationally defined by Lincoln and Guba (1985) as a method to develop rules for inclusion and category properties that form a basis for later tests of replicability and consistency.

The process used for identifying categories was as follows:

1. A card was selected from the collected pile, was read, and its contents noted. This first card represented the first entry in the first yet-to-be-named category. It was placed to one side.

2. The second card was selected, was read, and its contents noted. A determination was made either on tacit or intuitive grounds as to the similarity or difference than Card 1. If it was essentially similar to Card 1, it was placed with that card. If it was different, this card represented the first card in a yet-to-be named second category.

3. The process continued with each successive card. For each card, it was determined if the card was similar or different than the cards already read. The cards were placed with the other cards or a new category was made, as appropriate.

4. A card may have been read which did not fit any of the categories heretofore identified. This necessitated the formation of a new category designated for miscellaneous units of analysis.

5. Once the cards reached a critical mass (usually fifteen or sixteen) in a category, a prepositional statement was written for the properties that seemed to characterize the similar cards in the category. Each of these names captured the essence of the category and would serve as a rule for inclusion against which future cards could be compared. A review of each of the cards in a category against the rule of inclusion ensured their appropriate placement.

6. As subsequent cards were examined against the numerous rules for inclusion, they were assigned to categories on the basis of fit to the rule. If there were conflicts, anomalies, or inadequacies, a new category might emerge.

7. When the pile of cards containing units of analysis were exhausted, a review of the cards in the miscellaneous category were reviewed to determine if they would fit in the various categories or if they were unrelated to any of the other cards. Full sets of cards in categories were reviewed to determine if they were appropriately placed, if they needed to be placed in another category, or if they fit in two categories equally well. If they could fit in two categories, a duplicate card was made and placed in the second category.

8. The cards were reviewed for relatedness, that is, categories which were so closely related that one set of categories was a subset of another. They were then included for analysis together. A detailed description of this categorization process is found in Appendix D. Data in subsequent interviews were compared to the categories using the process described above. The constant comparison of units of analysis on the cards generated the theoretical properties of each category. In

reading each card contained in the category, I was able to see patterns and trends in the comments which had been made by the women This involves an interpretive process, not only in the placement of cards into the appropriate categories but also in the review of the common descriptions contained in the categories. The new patterns which are generated from this comparative analysis represent the theoretical properties of the categories, a theory arising from data.

The data generated from the women in this study were grouped into twelve categories: demographic information, childhood experiences, relationships these women had with others, issues related to business startup, barriers to starting business, personal goals, the awareness of their learning needs, what and how they learn, and the impact that they have on others. A description of the categories which emerged from the interviews in this study and their associated rules for inclusion is located in Appendix E.

As the interview process unfolded, the units of analysis and their inclusion into categories reflected the appropriateness of the categories. The first sets of interviews provided the initial categories and subsequent interviews either expanded the rules for inclusion or necessitated the development of new categories. Appendix F shows the interview units of analysis and their corresponding inclusion in the categories. This matrix illustrates the contributions of each woman in the interview in a particular category. (Each "x" represents a unit of analysis).

FOLLOW-UP WITH SUB-SAMPLE OF PARTICIPANTS

After the completion of the research interviews, eleven of the women who participated in the study were contacted by telephone to re-interview and review the overall findings. Several women expressed pleasure that I contacted them again and were very much interested in the overall findings of the research. Among those contacted and with whom I had post-research contact were Georgia Roberts, Paula Goodman, Dana Johnson, Lil Kohler, Cammy Hargrove, Marta Garza, Ann Mills, Eliza Brady, Judy Gage, Belinda Watkins, and Caren Thomas.

During our brief telephone conversations, I explained what had been found in the research and asked for their perspective on these findings. As I had done during the member checks during the interviews,

I asked the women what their perceptions were of these findings and whether they had additional comments or observations. The women responded overwhelmingly that the findings were interesting, accurate, and representative for them.

SUMMARY

This study used a naturalistic inquiry approach to define and describe the phenomenon of learning as it applies to the woman entrepreneur's acquisition of leadership skills. The sample consisted of eighteen women CEO's and Presidents from Texas, who are actively involved in the day-to-day operations of their businesses. One-on-one personal interviews were conducted with the women entrepreneurs, either in their work environment or in a restaurant or cafe near their work site. Demographic data were collected to discover similarities and differences among these women. The data were analyzed using a process of comparative categorization. Patterns and trends generating from interpretation of the data defined theoretical properties of twelve categories, which explain the phenomenon of learning for the participant group. The content of the data is presented as research findings in Chapter Four. The connections and emergent patterns of these findings are presented in Chapter Five.

IV

The Data

INTRODUCTION

The purpose of this research was to explore the phenomenon of learning of successful women entrepreneurs as described by the women themselves, a group of Texas business women: what they learned and how they learned in their lives. Further, I was interested in exploring the acquisition and enhancement of leadership skills among these women and in how they described this process. The research population consisted of eighteen female entrepreneurs who own Texas businesses with gross revenues of over $1 million and with over ten employees. The study used an unstructured interview methodology.

This study was not an analysis of the effectiveness of the learning or the effectiveness of the leadership skills of those interviewed.

RESEARCH PROTOCOL

The women participants were asked two basic questions:

1. How did you get to your current position as the CEO/President of this organization?
2. What do you do in your role as the head of this organization?

The first question enabled the interviewee to trace the behaviors and actions that they had undertaken in the past that led them to their present role as the business leader. The second question focused the entrepreneur on the behaviors and practices in her current role. Both questions employed an ethnobiographical approach to collecting the research data. The data obtained were rich in historical perspective: most of the women traced the kinds of activities and experiences of the past, often starting their biography with their childhood. Through the "story" of these entrepreneurial women's lives, I was able to derive information about their families, the role of childhood experiences which shaped their attitudes and behaviors, the significant relationships in their lives, their previous work experiences and startup of their current business, their personal goals and values, and knowledge of self as these all related to the way they led and learned in their organizations.

The "telling ourselves a story about ourselves" is an important element of feminist research, deriving theory from the experiences of the interview (Cotterill and Letherby, 1993). The narrative technique, such as the one used in this research, allows respondents to "tell the story" in whichever way they choose, and "importantly, validates individual experience and provides a vehicle through which this experience can be expressed to a wider audience (*Ibid*, p. 74).

The women in this study were open in discussing their life stories. I believe the content was honestly delivered and that the frankness of these women is testimony to the validity of their input. Two of the women spoke of how they had compromised their own sense of ethics and one woman spoke of the confidential nature of her company's growth plans ("off the record"). The interviews were characterized by a good deal of "run-on" or stream of consciousness discussion as the women talked about themselves, with an occasional interruption or interjection from me in support of their discussion.

I indicated at the start of the interview that, although I was not using a long list of research questions, I would engage the interviewee for elaboration or explanation of any points which might merit further exploration. These questions were spontaneous and based on the information provided during the interview. They were questions of clarification, i.e. "Could you describe what that first job was like?" and since they were situational for each interviewee, they were not uniformly postulated.

The research identified how these women have engaged in learning throughout their lives to acquire skills not only in leadership but in other aspects of their lives as well. The women followed a model of learning from experience: they clearly could define experiences that provided foundations for their future actions. The women were also self-directed in that clear patterns emerged in the analysis of how they have taken the responsibility to learn on their own with little or no external direction.

The following analyses are based on data acquired from the interviews. The first set of data presented provides demographic information, which was gathered in the interview. The data examining the phenomenon of learning in the researched group follows the demographic data.

DEMOGRAPHIC DATA

The women in this study ranged in age from 34 to 77 years of age at the time of their interview. Eleven of the women were in their forties. The women either volunteered their age readily during the course of the interview or broadly made references to the decade of their age.

The women in the interview supplied demographic information relative to their birth order and family structure. Eight of the women interviewed for this study were first born or sole child of their family. The women in this study primarily came from families with intact nuclear families, where the mother was a homemaker and the father was sole provider of financial support. A widower father raised one entrepreneur with support from a paternal grandmother and another was raised by a divorced mother who completed graduate work while the participant was a young child. For these entrepreneurial women, there was no single parent who exerted special influence: most spoke of strong mothers and fathers and one spoke of a role model aunt. Of the group, seven had siblings who were successful professionals or executives in other organizations. Three of the women started their businesses in the same field or industry as their father or father and mother; only one of the women had an entrepreneurial parent.

Of the women in the study, fifteen had been or were married, thirteen had children, and six had children who joined their mother's business as either employees or executives.

The women described their family backgrounds as follows:

I grew up in a household with a mother who is a schoolteacher (I was the oldest child) and a father who was a machinist in Massachusetts, who had to have a second job to be able to put us through school. My mother always taught first or second grade so she was always home . . . just a real blue collar background, church on Sundays, be good to the neighbors. It's a town of 25,000, Gloucester, Massachusetts, still 25,000 today.

There were four of us; I was the youngest, by a lot of years. It was almost like being the only child . . . My parents farmed . . . sharecropped a farm most of my life.

I was the oldest of five children. I grew up in a town of about 1,500 people in the middle of Kansas, very isolated. There are now five generations growing up in that town, so everybody is related. My parents are typical blue-collar workers . . . My parents are both hard workers, neither one of them being educated, both of them dropped out of school. They are not lower middle class; they are probably in the lower class. My mother and dad were very young, they were raising themselves and they had other children.

I come from a large family in a very small town and from a family that was prominent. I would say that everyone in my family was pretty ambitious. Having been raised as Southern ladies, the girls in my family, my sisters and I, several of us, by circuitous routes to realizing how ambitious. In my family, we had an attorney, two doctors, a college professor, a speech pathologist, and a software manager for a major database, a company president, and I have a sister who is still in graduate school undergoing a transition right now.

My father was the supervisor of a lumberyard back home. I have a sister older (47), I'm 44, and I have a brother that is 8 years younger, and I have a sister that is 10 years younger. The tradition that my family was as a Hispanic family, my father was very secure as a man and was not the macho man, pushing, resisting, and controlling. The macho picture was insecurity. I always explain that my father was very secure.

My dad was an agronomist with the University of Florida, a full professor but he never taught his first class until the late '60's. He had been in research basically. He taught an occasional class period but he never taught a whole semester long class. And my mother was a full-time housewife. It was . . . we were a family of the 50's. Father goes to work, doesn't earn a lot of money but makes enough to keep the family together. Mother stays home, takes care of the children, in our case it was four girls instead of three boys . . . er, two boys (referring to "Ozzie and Harriet" television show).

I'm a third generation real estate-oriented individual.

My father was a laborer. He did milking for farms for most of his life. And, in the later part of his life, he worked as a construction worker. Mom was a homemaker. All of my family comes from a very poor background, in fact, most of our relatives are in Monterrey (Mexico). And, that's where I was born.

My family's background was working class. I come from, my mother's side, my grandfather worked for Humble Oil, worked on the tank farm, and there were four daughters on my mother's family and my father was the son of two Polish immigrants, and his father was killed when he was eight months old. And so, they were both good-hearted people, they wanted better for me. Of the eight cousins, there were seven boys and myself on the Southern side; that's where my father wound up living, because my grandmother's bar and restaurant place was in Brooklyn in a rough neighborhood and he adopted the South. I was the only child.

I am the youngest of five; my husband is the oldest of five. I had a sister who was domineering, I had three big brothers who loved my sister and I to death and told us what we could do, and who we could date.

My mother was a certified lab technician, she had also gone to Rice and met my father and they got married . . . Unfortunately, my father dropped dead at 36 with a major heart attack which had a major impact on my mother, a widow with four kids. He was a chemical and a mechanical engineer out of Rice University and when he passed away, he was designing and manufacturing the heat shield to the Apollo capsule. I was thirteen, oldest of the four.

My mom is a behavioral psychologist so I had a lot of motivational research done on me -- achievement motivation, natural motivation skills. Just vicariously from living with her.
She had worked with Tina Horner, Rosabeth Moss Kanter, superstars; she was getting her Ph.D. with Bryn

Mawr. My father was an executive vice president with
Company X; he retired just this year.

Formal Education

Of the women interviewed for this study, four participants had
completed a baccalaureate degree in a "traditional" post high school
model. One subsequently completed an MBA at the University of Texas in
an Option II program which enables full-time employment during
matriculation. Another entrepreneur had a doctorate in linguistics and had
taught at a state university in the linguistics department. One participant
had a baccalaureate degree awarded by a university in Austin, which
granted extensive credit for life experiences and successful completion of
coursework. Another returned to a four-year institution to complete a
degree after a divorce and being primary caretaker for two children. Nine
of those interviewed did attend a four-year university or college for no
more than two years. One participant did not complete high school but did
attain a GED. The remaining three did not attend post high school formal
education.

Business Background

The women in the study were business owners in a variety of
industries. Only one woman could be said to be in an industry that was
predominantly populated by women: she was the owner of a beauty-related
organization. She met the criteria for the study and had developed a large
organization, one that is unique for the level of quality related innovations.
Three of the women were in the computer industry: one business
owner had been trained as a nurse but now had changed to the technical
world of computers. Another was in the technical field of software
development. A third was the head of a semiconductor-related
manufacturing business. These women had had training in computer
applications for both software and hardware. These three women had
received accolades from the Austin Business Community for their
successes in entrepreneurial endeavors; in fact, they were awarded
"Entrepreneur of the Year" over three different years.
Seven of the women were in businesses that they believed to be
heavily dominated by male business owners: one woman was a
commercial builder and another was in a metal services firm supplying to
the construction industry. The owner of a construction site/street barricade

and light business was included in the study as was a woman whose business manufactures and distributes slip rings for diverse uses as in petroleum rigs, helicopter rotors, and submarine trailing sounding devices. Two women owned businesses that repaired and supplied equipment to the communications industry: the owner of an electronics business and the owner of a communications headset business. Another woman included in the study owned and developed a plumbing, air conditioning and heating firm.

Two women were the chief executives and presidents of retail businesses that are expanding through franchise distribution: a back-related products store spreading through the United States and an ice cream store with seven locations expanding into the coffee products arena. The remainder of the group were in professional services: a woman who had a copying and reproduction business, a personnel services business, a real estate full-service business, an office supply distributor, and a public relations and advertising business owner. The public relations and advertising owner was awarded "Entrepreneur of the Year" in San Antonio, Texas for 1993.

Ethnicity Background

Two of the interviewees were Hispanic women of Mexican-American heritage; the rest were non-minority Caucasians. Nine of the women were born in Texas and had lived in the state most of their adult lives.

RESEARCH FINDINGS

The methodology used in this research study allows the areas of significance to emerge from the interview process. The phenomenon of learning for this group of businesswomen can be described as having four fundamental constructs: learning is a constant process in the lives of these women, on-going, and very much self-directed; personal experiences, learning from others, and learning by doing are the foundations of learning for the women in this study; the focus of their learning endeavors is two-fold: (1) to continually define their sense of self and (2) to solve business-related problems, to gain information which will assist them in operating their business, and to assist them in being better leaders; and the reliance on relationships and connectedness with others is integral to their learning process.

For these entrepreneurial women, the pattern of learning started in their childhood years. They recount experiences, which developed a strong sense of being unique or different from others, a strong values and belief orientation, and a strong interest in business-related activities. They were rewarded and reinforced for these learnings in their childhood and again in their ventures in the world of work. As they worked for others, they learned more about themselves, their capabilities and strengths, gathering information about not only how to accomplish the task but also how to work with people, building relationships and the foundation for their future endeavors. As they started their own businesses, they relied on their previous learnings and built upon them. They drew upon their internal motivation and their abilities to network and call upon resources in people they know to solve problems that they face in their role as leaders. They did not look for solutions through independent means: they relied on relationships and connections. They are most apt to call upon a spouse (with business expertise), a friend or mentor cultivated through business, or a business association for assistance or guidance in solving their dilemma. Their learning is, more often than not, spontaneous, just-in-time, and unplanned.

These women are faced with continuing the success of their businesses. For some, this means selling the business and trying a new endeavor, for others, continuing to grow their current enterprise. The learning activities they are engaged in as business owners are often related to their own business but also related to helping others--specifically, other women who they view as needing assistance to succeed in the business world. Hence, they view themselves not as receiving learning but passing on the benefits of what they have learned through their experiences. These women display characteristics of self-determinism and self-directedness: they are responsible for creating their own future and learning how to get there while taking responsibility to ensure that others get there, too.

Childhood Experiences

Many of the women started their interview with a chronicle of their life experiences from childhood on to adulthood. In doing so, they described incidents that occurred in their childhood that influenced their development of self-concept, that formulated their values and belief systems, and that shaped their orientations toward business and life's work. In nearly all incidents described, the recollections of their childhood experiences often included stories about a father or a mother or a significant other. From the start, then, they were influenced and affected by someone else and they had a positive relationship with that other person.

> My dad! He was very strict. He was very generous and he was very strict, he was like a philosopher. The times I've spent with my dad had a lot to do with the way I saw life and he was always like, "get on out there, get on out there." Then, when I would get out there, he would also go, "Wait, come back, come back." Because he could feel me slipping away a lot faster than my younger brother and sisters.

> I think I was following her (aunt): she was so glamorous and so beautiful and wore beautiful clothing, fabulous red hair, and I said, 'That's who I want to be like,' so I always patterned myself after my mother's sister who was in the beauty industry.

> My momma died when I was three and my two sisters were four years older and eight years older than me . . . our family encouraged the hugging. If you went to bed without being kissed, I guarantee you, you were madder than the devil and Daddy would come up and say, 'why is this light on?' and he would see you were awake and he would give you a kiss.

> My daddy could also sew a fine seam, he could out-crochet and out-knit anybody in the family.

> My mother was incredible. Her four daughters were probably as different as four daughters growing under the same roof could be. Yet she gave each one of us tremendous encouragement to be what we want.

The women's memories included doing things with a parent sharing a part of their world with the daughter and involving the child in the parent's work. This demonstration of special attention had positive effects on the young girls:

> My most prideful moments that I could remember was my mom getting me a pass so I could walk down from

the elementary school to meet her at lunch. I remember feeling so important that I was going to have lunch (with her) and so proud that my mom worked. That was at a young age . . . My mom wouldn't leave us at any time. We were in Washington, D.C. because she was at a psychologists' conference. We got to stay in a hotel and it was so much fun watching the soaps and all.

My daddy took me everywhere he went that was interesting.

In the interview, several women described themselves as being the only child in the family interested in the parent's work and how they regarded it as "fun." This reinforced a sense of uniqueness and specialness in the young girl, as distinctly different than their siblings:

My two oldest sisters weren't interested in doing things
            . . . I can remember one night in total: He (the father) said to me at dinner one night, 'Tomorrow is Saturday. Would you have time to help me "right" two joints?' And I said, 'Sure.' My sister said, 'What are you talking about? What do you mean, "joints"?' I said, 'Daddy, you tell her.' He was talking about putting joints together under the commode and it was kind of fun because I got to see things that a man did and most daughters don't get a chance for that.

I was a bit precocious. My father would take me, after he made lumber and window deliveries, to certain places where they were building something. I would always look and say, 'that's where the wall goes up,' 'that's where the window is.' I was seven and I could measure a room. No one else in my family would trail along with him.

I have done everything in this business. I've built barricades; I've changed lights. My entire teen-age years were spent sitting in the garage on a Sunday afternoon fixing lights with my dad. So I really have come from the bottom up.

In addition to feeling "different" because they were interested in their parent's work, being "different" manifested itself in a variety of ways as described by the women.

> It was like, uh, I never considered myself to be pretty or all-American. As I look back, I can see that my coloring was different (than others in my family) and I knew for sure that I was going to be something someday . . . I knew that I was going to leave Franklin. I really didn't know what, but I knew that I would be in business. I didn't want to go to college. I didn't want to do anything but be in business.

> I had been in the third grade when I read Carnegie's *How to Win Friends and Influence People.* I was babysitting and the people I was babysitting for had the book; every time I went to babysit, I read the book . . . Most first graders wouldn't have been reading Sylvia Porter's Money column either, and I had been doing that.

> I had a real, extreme aversion to having my parents support me. Literally, since I was about twelve, I bought my own groceries . . . My brother and I were always cared for but if we chose to make certain decisions for ourselves, that meant you had to pay for it. It was a long story but my mom really instilled independence in us because both my parents were depression children and had a strong work ethic.

> Part of this decision making process that I went through as a young adult had to do with deciding that I was smart, that I could do anything I wanted to. I don't know that others do that.

> My parents are typical blue-collar workers. They, my dad would get paid on Friday and on Monday, they were broke. They didn't have anything and I swore when I was ten years old that I wasn't going to live this way . . . I made the remark to my mother when I got to be eighteen or when I got out of school that I was going to have a new home and a new car so I could drive down

the street. My mom said, 'And I suppose that will be a
Cadillac?' and I said, 'At least.'

So, right away, I suppose that I felt different, I possibly
felt like, alone. I think in feeling that way, knowing you
are different to start with and then being told a lot that
you are different, you begin to, first of all, you don't put
up a lot of shields, kind of like a self-protection type of
thing. It will have you be very outgoing also, like you
start covering sometimes with a lot of bravado and
boisterousness just getting out there. And, that's what I
did for years. When I got to high school, the only thing I
kept, was keeping me in high school was the
extracurricular activities and my dad.

I had the notion that I wanted to be in Greenwich
Village. I was a beatnik at heart. And, you know, things
haven't really changed. I'm still there, liking different
things.

I quit school at the ripe old age of fifteen and got married
so I only have a ninth grade education. But, I have
always had drive.

In some cases, being "different" related to being directive or assuming a
leadership position:

I led at a very young age. I was always the president of
the family. I was always the boss. I was always the
president of everything. I mean, if one of my siblings
had a slumber party, I butted in and we had to have a
'sing along.' This is just the way I was born.

I was in college when my father died and I knew I
needed to go home and be the main support for my
family. I had always been the 'baby' but now there was
newer 'babies' and I was the only one who could work.
I think that even as a child, I always was an adult; I liked
to do adult things. My parents let me make decisions.

I was very different than my siblings. I think I was first
conscious of that after my father passed away because I

realized that we could not spend our whole lives mourning that fact. We had to go on and realize that he would have wanted that.

Being "different" also meant excelling in a circumstance where others may have traditionally failed. Ann Mills said

> In my senior year of high school, I worked 36 hours a week waitressing. I stored up a lot of cash. The last nine weeks, I missed six weeks out of nine weeks of class and still got straight A's. They had to call my mother into the school because this did not track with their picture. I was supposed to be failing. What could they say? I wasn't the norm.

The to-be entrepreneur could also relate anecdotes that demonstrated an early interest in doing business-related things. Georgia Roberts talked about two of her childhood moneymaking projects:

> When I was little, one of the ways that I used to earn money was to loan money to people at usurious interest rates because my sisters and my friends never had any money but I always did. Because I didn't spend money; I still don't. I bought a savings bond with my own money when I was five years old. I remember we went down to the post office, my dad went with me. It cost $18.25 to buy a $25 war bond (at that time they were still calling them war bonds instead of savings bonds). I remember I could just barely see the man, and he wanted to put my dad's name on it and I was furious. And I just gave him a piece of my mind. My father had had nothing to do with my earning this money and he was not going to get any of it.

As youngsters or teens, several women had positive experiences that influenced their work attitudes.

> When I was fifteen, I went to work in Arby's roast beef. I was their youngest employee. I loved working there. Loved learning about that business and doing an excellent job. I made artistic things and sold them at art fairs. I was always working from when I was real small.

> I had one business venture after another from the time
> that I was five years old on. By the time I was seven, I
> had been written up twice in our town newspapers about
> my business ventures. One was for the soda fountain; the
> other was for the circus. I had had a day camp for
> children ages six to twelve that I had run for three years
> after I graduated from high school that had put my sisters
> and I through college. It was even written up in
> Seventeen magazine for that matter.

Youth work experiences were not necessarily need-driven for those who
did engage in work, but it was for Judy Gage who grew up in a small town
in Kansas:

> I was always extremely independent even at a young age.
> I basically supported myself in high school and worked
> year round, held two jobs . . . I had to work to go to high
> school. My parents could not afford to buy my books, my
> clothes, so I had to do that, too.

It is clear from the interview data that many of the women could relate
specific incidents that demonstrated ways that their parents influenced
their current beliefs and value system development, especially around
learning, independence, and self-ability.

> My father did things, prior to him dying, as he was quite
> successful. I will never forget one Christmas. We
> walked past an alley in Chicago, and there was a guy
> living in a cardboard box, y'know a refrigerator box and I
> was just thinking, 'this is terrible, this is horrible.' See, I
> was morally horrified and the, uh, he took me down to
> the cardboard box and introduced himself to the man in
> the cardboard box, who in retrospect was probably three
> sheets to the wind. We started talking to this guy and
> uh, I forgot exactly what he had done, but it was a Wall
> Street broker or lawyer or something like that. We ended
> up standing in that alley and talking to that guy for
> almost an hour. And, when we came out of there, my
> father said to me, 'Never forget that you never judge
> people by how they look or where they live or what they
> are even doing specifically in only that moment in time.

Every person has something to teach you and you must be open.' I can tell you what the cardboard box looked like, what he looked like. . . I learned some things.

My father felt that the worse possible sin was not to live up to your potential or not to be able to cross the threshold of a dream and make it reality.

From Caren Thomas came this comment about her father:

From now on, when I look back (the older you get, the more you look back), my father was really a role model/mentor. Good sense of humor, caring individual. The person who said, 'I know you could get a scholarship to school if you wanted, but that would deprive someone else of a scholarship, so you can work and we will work and that's how we will do it.'

Lisa Bollcher also was strongly influenced by her dad:
I was close to my dad. And my dad always told us, 'You can do anything you want to do.' And I'd say, 'But daddy, I can't make this bolt move.' He said, 'You haven't got the right leverage on it. Think about how to get more leverage on it. You can do it.' And then he would walk off. Or he'd say, 'You fell and hurt yourself on the shovel that you've been digging this hole with. Get to the house and fix it.'

Eliza Brady talked about her parents' influence as well:

My parents, particularly my father, placed an emphasis on reputation, reputation being how you treated other people, how responsible you were, keeping your word, and whether you did the right thing, so I had that kind of upbringing at an early age.

Other comments made by the women regarding familial influences included:

I remember when I went to Cornell in New York City, coming home on a plane. Eastern Airlines had a survey to ask you how much your parents made and I really didn't know how much my father made, and so, I asked him when I got home. He said, 'Is there anything in life you really, really needed that you haven't had?' I said, 'No.' Then he said, 'Then it makes no difference what I make for a salary.' So, you can see, based on that, proud. Plus, money wasn't the goal in life.

And my father would be saying today, 'Don't ever get too big for your britches.'

We're a very close family, with my siblings. I give a lot of credit to my parents, to my mother for teaching to be loving, showing love, that you have to earn people's respect, you just don't get it. It's what this country is all about.

My mother was incredible. Her four daughters were probably as different as four daughters growing under the same roof could be. Yet she gave each one of us tremendous encouragement to be what we want.

We were definitely not, uh, flush with money. It was not a soft upbringing. A lot of the values I have today are because of the way I was raised.

The women in the study related how external reinforcement and praise provided an encouragement to continue the endeavors that demonstrated their uniqueness:

I had picked out several books I'd like to read and went to the librarian's desk to check them out. She peered down and here I am, not even able to peer up the counter. She looked at these books and looked at me and asked, 'How old are you?' I said, 'Five.' She asked, 'Can you read these books?' I said, 'Yes.' She opened one up and I started to read it. She opened another and I started to read it. She opened another, and I read it, too. She said, 'Okay.' She asked me my name, made out all the paperwork and she checked the books out to me. From that point on, I could check out anything I wanted.

> I would say that being in the middle (of the family) gave me a lot of encouragement to go and do what I wanted to do.

> I had one business venture after another from the time I was five years old on. By the time I was seven, I had been written up twice in our town newspapers about my business ventures.

Post-Childhood Experience (Prior to Own Business Startup)

Following the discussion of their childhood experiences, the women interviewed generally spoke of either pursuing their baccalaureate studies or their first experiences working for others. Of the eighteen women in this study, eleven entered college upon completing high school and seven subsequently left college to enter the work force or get married, without completing their degree.

Eliza Brady was one of those who had entered college immediately after high school. She expressed a lack of focus and genuine goals while in school:

> I didn't have any aspirations career wise. As a teenager, a college student, it never really occurred to me that I would work. I just never even thought about it . . . I ran off and went to California at the age of 19 after cramming two years of college into a year and a half.

This was echoed by Marta Garza, the owner of a construction firm:

> When I went to college, I didn't know what I wanted to do. To tell you the truth, some people have it all together, but in my generation, we never knew from one day to the next, what was available for us, what was allowed. No one ever said, 'Why don't you become an engineer?' No one ever said that to me. There were a number of reasons for non-completion of college.

Both Georgia Roberts and Judy Gage went to work to support a husband through college.

> When I quit college, I was working in the bank and I got
> married and we moved to Kansas City. My husband was
> going to school and one of the reasons why I quit school
> was that one of us had to work, so I quit school and put
> him through school.

> I worked all the way through my husband's graduate
> school.

Two of the women interviewed left college to assist their families through
a family crisis. This further developed the self-esteem and sense that
others depended on them.

> I came back to Texas . . . my family was having a lot of
> health and emotional problems and I came back, I've
> always been the person in my family who was the
> troubleshooter, uh, not necessarily right, but definitely
> respected.

Dana Johnson said,

> I went to the University for about three years and was
> bored beyond belief. Yes, I made straight A's. I loved
> biology, I've always been competitive, I've always loved
> reading and learning, but I also, at the time, wanted to
> make money and accomplish things. It was just too
> difficult to stay in college.

Lisa Bollcher went back to school as an older student and completed her
baccalaureate as a divorced mother of two. Maria Garcia went back to
school but did not complete her degree.

> I tried it in--what year was that--'78 or '79. I decided
> that I needed to do something and so I went back. Took
> two semesters. I just didn't have, and maybe it was
> because I had to go back to the basics. I didn't have time
> for that.

One of the most significant learnings that these women had
around the topic of formal education was that they learned that they could
succeed in spite of not having a degree. The prevalent attitude expressed
in the interviews is that the lack of a baccalaureate degree did not hinder

them in their subsequent endeavors. They believe that formal education was not a requisite to success in their field:

> It doesn't take an education, it doesn't take a degree, it takes just hard work, common sense and the energy to want to carry through. That's what it takes. I guess if I had a degree, it would have been easier for me, I would have applied skills there to carry this business faster. But I don't think that's the overall ingredient.

> The largest problem we have in America is that formal education is not always designed to help the person learn how to make a living. Somebody needs to change the system so that it is more of an apprenticeship, not require a degree in something that is worthless. I don't need a degree to make a living as a general contractor.

> I don't think you can find a person that went to college knowing that they were going to own and operate a full service real estate company. There isn't any such thing. You don't go to school and learn how to own and operate.

> It is not the answer for everybody. If I went back and got a degree, great. I'd get a degree in English, in history, and I could go teach. I don't need it. What we say in construction is that you learn by hard knocks. I have.

> There are still lots of things that I don't know about business. When I was starting the business, there was almost everything I didn't know about it. I had taken some business courses in college but I didn't remember anything from them.

> I could have gone and took a course and I'd have been doing a lot of running back and forth . . . I would have gotten in fifty hours, maybe two hours of something applicable to slip rings. Here (in her facility) I get it straight.

Belinda Watkins, owner of an electronics firm had completed three years of college and felt that this did contribute to her ability to deal with people:

My educational background is in hard sciences and I
switched mid-way through to the social sciences, so I had
a strong background in psychology which doesn't really
fit with electronics, but it was handy. It teaches you how
to deal with people.

The women who did not go to college experienced the world of
employment in a variety of organizational settings prior to establishing
their own businesses. In these different jobs, they continually developed
and learned about themselves and their capabilities. They showed a spirit
of competitiveness and drive:

When I was on the farm, I was picking cotton, milking
the cows; I did everything in my power to keep up with
the guys. When they went out at 8:00 in the morning, I
got there at 7:00 to get a head start and try to outdo
somebody else and worked my heart out all day. And I
could never be number one, because always one of the
guys could beat me. We got paid by the pound, I just
wanted to be the fastest.

Employment often meant working at a low-paying clerical type position:

I had about a year and a half of work behind me as a
clerk in a loan company so that's the extent of the
experience in business, *per se*.

Lisa Bollcher said:

I was doing good to find that dollar an hour job when I
got out of high school and jobs were hard to come by.
Minimum wage was a dollar an hour and that was it. I
mean, if you worked here and you did good, you might
get a nickel raise. When I got to $1.65, I was doing
books for a large size, a heating and air conditioning
warehouse type situation. From there, I went into
government. They didn't pay very good either. And so, I
worked in a lot of purchasing departments, accounting
departments, and they call you this or that or the other,
but you just didn't make any money. I think I was
making $2.50 an hour when I finally decided to go into

real estate and within three years, I was making $25,000 a year.

Eliza Brady, when faced with divorce and the need to support two small children, recognized she had to do something to find employment.

> So, here I was a 24 year old young lady who had not been seriously trained in anything except how to make polite conversation suddenly needing a job that would support three people.

This was repeated by Kate Hammond:

> I was on the political out, my research project was canceled, I had ailing parents, I was the only child, I had teenage children and one of them was going through a rough time, and I realized that I needed to keep bringing in roughly the same amount of compensation . . . either that or dramatically change our lifestyle. So it was, um, you know, I thought 'can I do anything but this?'

This desire to improve one's economic situation was impetus for Karen Lewis as well:

> I worked in the metal service industry and the first job I had I started as a bookkeeper and I worked for a man for several years and then I changed to another competitor, you know, always because they offered me more money anyway.

Caren Thomas had graduated with a nursing degree and had practiced nursing in California spoke about her move to Texas:

> I didn't do any nursing in Texas because you took a fifty per cent pay cut from California to Texas. My feeling was I worked for five years for my degree from Cornell and I wasn't happy to be making even less than some grocery store checkers, so I went on and did volunteer work and meals on wheels.

Kate Hammond, the sole Ph.D. in the interviewed group, expressed her desire for economic improvement as follows:

> I had taught for ten years and had made the transition to computer sciences because I wanted mobility and money. Teaching's fine, but in the discipline I was in, there weren't the opportunities I wanted.

The experience of looking for employment that was suitable led one woman to learn about herself and the means to which she would use to keep her family fed. Eliza said:

> I heard about this job . . . in a restaurant/bar and so I took her (my sister's) credentials. I decided in my process that if I had to lie to get a job, I would. I'd figure it out when I got there but the main thing was that I had to get a job. Well, I'll tell you, it's the only time that I've done that but I absolutely did. Hardly anything on my resume was true.

This woman wasn't the only one to learn about herself. Lil Kohler, who was employed at a Fortune 500 technical and engineering firm and who had worked her way up from hourly employee to first woman manager, told a story of how she was persistent and rewarded for standing up for herself:

> I went down and talked to (my supervisor) and said, 'I want this job.' And he said, 'You know that "'Jim Baker"' won't let me hire a woman.' I knew that was the reason but I'd never had anyone ever come out and tell me the reason. And so, being the brazen person I was, I just went down to 'Jim Baker,' the Division Manager, and waited right there until he would see me. I went and talked to him and told him I wasn't asking for anything but the opportunity and if I couldn't make it, they could just go back and send me back to the line. But, I was tired of them hiring guys and sending them up to me to train.

She did get the position and went on to run chip sales, an entrepreneurial division within this company (in fact, the most profitable division in the entire company).

Working in the companies belonging to others gave these women an opportunity to learn and refine different attitudes and skills, which they would use later when they started their own businesses.

> I was a bookkeeper and then I later went into advertising and real estate and things like that.

> So I left the university at twenty and opened Henry S. Miller's Commercial Research office when they first came here from Dallas. I went into research for about a year. I stayed in research in a salaried position . . . then I went free lance and called on commercial companies and did their research, brochure work, syndications, all that kind of stuff. And decided that I could have a whole lot of fun selling these things. And I went into commercial sales and I stayed in commercial sales with a company in San Antonio.

> The key for a woman to be truly happy in her success is to realize that she is a woman and be proud of it. We don't have to act like men . . . I look back in the mid 70's, just about every woman that I met in the electronics industry were trying to play the male role. They were trying to look male and they were trying to talk male. And they were trying to drink like a male. They had this stereotype that they needed to do the bar scene and belly up to the bar with the best of the men (if that's what you call men, and in my book, that's not what I call men), you know, it was sad to me. Sad to see what women were doing to their image when all they had to do was be themselves. That's all they had to do and that's all they have to do today.

> As a legal secretary, one of the primary thrusts (today what I did would actually be considered a legal assistant but in those days, they didn't have that terminology), one of the primary thrusts is that everything you turn out from a paperwork standpoint has to be absolutely perfect because the only advertising the attorneys could do was through the written product that left our office and so I learned to take a great deal of pride and caring about the

quality of the paperwork. So, good copies made real
good sense.

I knew some of the things about business when I started.
I knew accounting. I knew about payroll deductions and
I knew about taxes. I knew a little bit about marketing, a
lot about selling.

As I was in bookkeeping at that particular company, I
started talking to customers and started giving them
prices. Bookkeeping is okay but it is not near as fun as
sales. Sales is a fun job. You get very, I don't know,
involved. You get really exhilarated when you get an
order, it's really an upper. Especially if you've got one
from somebody else.

For Kate Hammond, her background as a mother and Southern woman
prepared her for business:

I think part of it is, you raise a family on a teacher's
salary and you learn about money management, right?
And, uh, being a Southern woman teaches you a lot
about manipulation. Coming from behind makes you
tough.

Some of the things that the women learned were "don'ts" for their own
organizations. Lil Kohler talked about how her employment as the
General Manager of a company owned by someone else created an internal
struggle between her need for employment and her values.

We weren't doing things the way we should have been
doing them at Company T. We grew fast and we
compromised our quality and, uh, that was something we
never did at ABC Company. If you're compromising it,
you are compromising yourself. It got so I couldn't sleep
at night, so once again, I was losing weight very, very
rapidly, and I had a sense at that time that if I continued
at the rate at which I was going, with the stress that I
couldn't cope with, I would take myself right back to the
situation I had been in before. I made up my mind that
money was not real important to me, and that I was a
good waitress and I loved sales (and there was always

something out there for me to sell). So I gave my notice
. . . I had no idea of what I was going to do.

What she did was to contact former business associates, got commitments for sales of semiconductor parts, and started her own business. Her concern for quality led her to receive awards and commendations from her customers for her consistent delivery of quality parts.

Again and again, the women in the study discussed their experiences and how they learned from them. These experiences involved learnings with others. They either had mentors or role models, or they learned how to deal effectively with people, or they were given opportunities and supported by others to try new areas.

> They asked me if I wanted to go (and manage their startup). I left managing the restaurant. I still felt like I was going to go to medical school, but I'll just take this year to do this. I went to Manhattan and everything from helping to find the location, working with the architect to design the space, to hiring all the employees, finding all the suppliers, they let me work very creatively in all those areas, but they were there for support.

> I made really good money because it was such a busy place. It gave me enough money to get by for a little while and I could figure out what else to do.

> I started asking questions. 'Why am I doing this? Why is this bad? What am I looking for?' Well, it kind of surprised them because they had never been asked questions before, but most of the engineers kind of brushed me off, but there was this one guy, I'll never forget him as long as I live, his name was 'John Smith.' He had the patience of Job . . . He would sit there and draw me pictures of how they would develop the devices and how everything was made and how they would cut the windows out and have the emitters and everything. Hours, hours he spent with me, explaining it to me.

> You can't say it's too much work. Just get your butt moving and do it because it is to your advantage . . . It behooved me to work for people who were

procrastinators, who really didn't like to work, because I
did their hard work and learned.

He (her previous employer) brought in an outside CPA
who taught me bookkeeping in a week and how to do all
that stuff. So, I learned on that job all kinds of business
skills. I never had any higher math courses but I'm
finding that in a lot of work, I'm just using high school
math. That's all you use in accounting. So, I had
enough education to learn everything I had to learn and
in that job, I learned how to do job costing, payroll, client
contact, and technical writing.

As a kid, your parent tries to tell you, but you don't
realize that everything that you do every day of your life
is building your reputation and the people you come into
contact with's perception of who you are as a person.
That was just a culmination of people (who) believe in
me and they like my spark. That felt wonderful and just
that in itself was probably the most supportive.

All that being in the bank did for me was it gave me the
basis to be where I am today. It gave me the basis to
know that I could direct people. It certainly gave me the
accounting and the ability to organize . . . At the age of
25, I had fourteen employees working underneath me
that I was supervising at the bank, many of them being
much older than myself.

I had no experience in those work areas but I had a
strong work ethic, I'm very perceptive and so he just put
me in charge of it. If you need direction, he'd give you
some, but he just latches on to someone who was not
afraid of trying their ideas out.

I came out of ABC Company and they had so many good
programs and I learned so much when I was there. It's a
quality company, but I was 35146 while I was there, and
I will never forget that. I was a number. That's the last
thing I ever want our people to feel like they are. They
are part of the team.

My husband knew I could build houses. He really didn't want me to work because it would increase the amount of money we would pay in taxes. But, I told him it was an investment in my future. Instead of going to school, building houses was building my career.

I've loved every job I ever had and I learned so much from the people who ran the other company. People think that work is bad, that it's something that you struggle through for forty hours a week. Instead, it can be your playtime if you pick the right job and I want our employees to understand that.

When I went to work for these two women who owned a lot of property here in Austin, the good thing, the positive things that happened to me in my career, when I look at what I know is because whenever I went to work with somebody, either part time or whatever they needed me to do, I ended up taking over from their lack of interest or energy or you name it. The secret is hard work, learning at someone else's expense. They were responsible for the financial, to keep all the bills going. I was learning while they had the responsibilities.

When we started to get all the press in New York, they (the owners) were never profiled, they allowed me to be profiled. That was very generous of them. I always felt like that was the first Ann's Ice Cream.

I loved pretty much working for them, really wonderful, just that they had a lot of intuition about what motivated people. I don't know if they were really conscious about it, but functionally it worked very well for them.

There were role models in the work environment who significantly influenced the entrepreneur, someone who taught the to-be entrepreneur something. Lil Kohler had briefly sold home decorating products as a side job while working in a corporate environment, thinking that the sideline interest could be another field to enter. The leader of the home decorating company, Mary Crowley, was a contemporary of Mary

Kay Ash of Mary Kay Cosmetics fame, and would be an inspiration and mentor to Lil, who would later become an Entrepreneur of the Year.

> Mary, when she walked into a room, there was just an air about that woman. I never, and I listen to a lot of motivational speakers, all of them, but I never met anyone who could make you feel quite as good about yourself as a woman as Mary Crowley could . . . I think that Mary did so much that year. I changed the image of myself, she made me realize that there were so many things that I needed to do to improve myself because, up to that point, I had gone brute force, because it was the only way I knew how to go . . . I honestly believe that had it not been for that experience with Mary Crowley, I would not have had the nerve to start my company. But, when I started, I could think about the things that she did, the hard hours she had to overcome, and I thought, if she did, then I could do it.

Starting Their Businesses

The women in this study started their businesses at different points in their lives and with different levels of preparation. Most of the women started their businesses in response to a dramatic change in their lives; others took a more evolutionary approach. For those in the latter category, their own business was a natural step: they were employed in the same field and then decided to start their own enterprise. Through the whole process of starting their businesses, the women continued to learn and continued to rely on family members, close business friends, and mentors to assist them in the development of their organization.

For some entrepreneurs, starting a business was the result of seeking independence and autonomy:

> Obviously one of the reasons that women go into business for themselves is that they want to be their own boss, they don't want to work for somebody else anymore, be held back, or not be given the opportunity to prove that they can do it.

> So, I was miserable. I started doing some interviews, this other researcher and I got together and we asked,

'What could we do, what could we do in the software that had a big enough market and could make us independent?'

I had always had this envisionment (sic) that I was going to be my own boss. It's just--I had it all wrong. I didn't know it was going to be in office products. I thought it would be a hamburger stand or something. The reason why I started my own company was that that would give me the freedom to do exactly what I wanted to do.

I had been a legal secretary for many years and at the ripe old age of 28, I had reached the conclusion that I could never work for anyone else again as long as I lived. I was tired of being told, 'Georgia, don't worry your pretty little head about that,' or 'Georgia, just leave the business to the men' or 'Georgia, you're making very good money for a woman.' Those kind of comments just somehow did not sit quite right with me.

For Maria Garcia, the owner of a large office supply house, the timing of starting her business was unexpected: an opportunity materialized and she seized the moment.

One day I came in and the owner of a printing business was talking to his CPA and his CPA was telling him, 'Look, you've got to get rid of this inventory. It's nothing but dead weight, it's costing you money and you need that money for your print shop. So, get rid of it."' I catalogued it and the following day, I went back after my work and I said, 'So, you need to get rid of this, huh?' And he said, 'Yeah.' And I said, 'How much do you want for it?' He says, 'I don't know, I don't have any idea what it's worth. Make me an offer. Do you want it?' 'Yeah . . . I'll give you $1500.' He said, 'I'll take it.' It was not something that was planned, it just happened.

The same was true for the Georgia Roberts:

I eventually discovered the Relax the Back store that was located over at Hancock Drive at the time. An osteopath

started it in 1984. How I hadn't discovered it before, I'm
not really sure. Probably because I wasn't looking,
because it's not easy to find, and they apparently had no
advertising. And it wasn't doing very well. But it had a
lot of neat products and these products work! And I was
actually having less pain because of these products. I
decided I liked them and so I bought the business.

An unexpected start is also reflected in this comment from Karen Lewis:

The last man I worked for was a very, very difficult man
to work for and I got no cooperation in trying to figure
these costs. One day he said, 'I don't like your attitude.'
And I said, 'I don't like your attitude either. I'm gone.'
And I walked out the door. And I got home and went,
'What am I going to do now?'

Starting a business may have been the result of providing a needed service.

I just did a lot of listening to what people had to say at
the various parties. Over and over again, I'd hear these
complaints that there wasn't anyplace where you could
get decent copies made inexpensively around the
university. I thought that sounds like the kind of thing I
could do.

We were basically known as people who came out and
unstopped lines . . . We built this business because we are
emergency services, you don't wait two or three days for
us.

In corporations, it (creativity) is stifled even more.
Because there is such a thing as a bad idea, people will
make you feel stupid. At those big places, people pay
money for ideas because they're not allowed to have them
themselves. And it's a no-risk thing: 'Oh, Kay proposed
this, not me. I just thought I'd pass it along to you and
see what you thought.'

The head of the public relations and advertising firm had been employed at
another advertising firm when impending marriage to one of the partners

at the firm caused her to start her own company. Kay saw a problem in their new relationship:

> You know, we were going to get married and couldn't work for him anymore, because, you know, it's too weird. And I couldn't work for anybody else because he travels so much and I want to go with him, so really the only option was to go into business for myself which I had never really ever considered.

The importance of providing for family was the main impetus for starting a business for Paula who had followed her management-level husband through the moves required for his career with a telephone company.

> Our goal was to save money for our kids' college education.

Paula's family supported her new business, physically and through morale support.

> My husband was there, he was a career man. He was a very smart businessman and we started working on weekends. We brought our children in; our whole goal was to prepare for their college education. We brought our children in, they worked for us in the summer, they answered phones, they ran copies, whatever it took and then we would pay them.

Family support was also a critical dimension for Maria Garcia who could not get any financial loans to fund her new business until her father borrowed money against his home to help her out.

> My mother was a little bit skeptical, she said, 'I don't know about this.' My Dad sounded like--you know--he knew I was a hard worker and that whatever it was I was into I'd give it my best.

The confidence of the new entrepreneur comes through the following statements:

> I was twenty-four years old and thought I knew everything, um, started my own business and that was in 1976.

In 1971, I made the decision that I would just have to start my own business of some kind. I had no idea what I was going to start but I was going to start my own business.

I told my husband, 'I could do that better.' He'd say, 'You can do it better?' But I thought that I could.

Some of the women didn't have a clear plan in what they were going to do at the outset, but the same confidence in self comes through these comments:

And so, February 5, I found myself in business and not really knowing quite what to do.

At 11:00 that morning, I was in downtown L.A. trying to set up a corporation. I had no idea of what I was going to do or how I was going to set it up, but in two hours I had a corporation set up and we were incorporated on the 29 of July and I had the doors open on August 17.

I was forced by circumstances to arrive at some pretty hard decisions. And, I realized in that process, which I just kind of muddled through on my own, that I had been falling backwards in everything I had done. I had not set down and gone through a decision making process in anything that I had ever done. So, in a way, I kind of defaulted into everything. I mean, I made choices, but I had no good process for making them.

Starting one's own business was not without its share of challenges and crises.

Two university professors, one of them invested $1,200 and the other gave me $1,800, for a total of $3,000. The banks wouldn't even accept my loan applications. It wasn't that they wouldn't give me the loan--they wouldn't accept my applications. But I learned much later is that with $3,000 it was impossible to work and yet it did.

The trick is that they (the investors) like what they see or else they wouldn't give you money but, then, almost immediately at the time they write the check, there is this knot in their stomach about whether or not they did the right thing.

The people part is a real problem. I've had real bad luck in bookkeepers. I had a good gal and she transferred to Arkansas. So, I had about three or four, had good references, they couldn't add and they really didn't know what they were doing.

The day before I left TI, I went to see the doctor just to get my check up. Melonoma appeared on my neck.

I had a little bit of a problem in May of that same year. I got into an auto accident and totaled my parents' car. Ended up with a neck brace and couldn't work for about thirty days. Almost had to close the place down, but I was bound and determined that that wasn't gong to happen.

The women spoke of specific processes they underwent to learn the essentials necessary for business ownership. These processes involved getting professional help from a subject matter expert. These women did not go about learning these areas themselves; they valued the help of a professional and learned from them.

We went to the Small Business Administration, got a template for writing a business plan, picked up a bunch of prospectuses to find out how other people had written theirs. We borrowed legal documents from other companies to try to reduce our expenses. We did put together a good group of professionals, we hired an excellent attorney and an excellent accounting firm so we were not shoeboxing it.

I started doing research, you don't do anything without research. I had to get me a bonding agent, an insurance company, an attorney to draw up papers, and I went looking for those things. Here's what I want, this is what

I want to do. I've got $25,000 in cash to invest, help me
set it up right.

You use your resources, you ask questions. It's like
anything else. If you want to buy a house, nobody has
experience buying their first house. You figure out how
to do it. You figure out what your expenses are going to
be. You do research.

The new entrepreneur relied on relationships that she had previously made
to staff up her new business. The women would utilize the people in these
relationships to assist her in her operational activities or depend on them
for support and encouragement. These were people who knew the
capabilities of the woman, usually previous business associates, mentors
and family.

I had a set up of three employees, one of whom I hired at
the 7-ll 'cause he treated my children well. You could
hire University of Texas grads to start at $30,000 which
was probably more than I was paying myself, so I
decided that I would indeed find one and train him
myself.

I had $3,000 in savings, moved everything down here,
we wrote a business plan, raised $100,000, a guy who I
had worked with at Steve, who opened his own ice cream
shop called Company Z in Boston, gave me $5,000 and
sent me a note that said, "Here is $5,000. Send me some
stock when you get some." He is not a rich guy, he didn't
know what percentage he was getting in the company.
That gave us our seed capital. Enabled us, no one wants
to be the first.

Friends came out of the woodwork and put money in and
my old boss at ABC Company became one of them. That
was quite a vote of confidence, I felt.

Maria Garcia received assistance from a generous subject matter expert
who had had experience with her prior to her starting her business.

So, all of a sudden this gentleman CPA comes in and I
said, 'Here is what we've done and we've done this.' And

he said, 'Well, here's what you need to do.' And he kind
of listed everything--and he said that I needed to get my
ID and he gave me some guidelines for accounting and
he didn't charge me because he knew I didn't have the
money. And he told me I needed a bank account, so all in
that same day, I went and I set up a bank account, I went
to get my ID number.

The Current Role: Woman Business Owner

In their current position, the women in this study had overcome
many of the challenges associated with the startup of a new business and
were concerned with growing their organizations. The skills they used to
bring their businesses to this point were developed and refined in prior
work experiences, they had learned what they needed to do to be
successful, what worked and what did not work.

A significant part of the "how I got here" is credited to their
strong sense of personal identity. This personal identity was one of
someone who was different and unique, who could control her own destiny
and who could handle whatever came her way--she would make things
happen. This strong sense of personal identity contributed to their ability
to start their businesses and to be successful in overcoming adversities and
meeting challenges head on. Their belief in their abilities and skills was a
learned response: they met challenges in the past and they had faith in
their ability to handle whatever came their way.

When people talk about being lucky, I believe very much
in luck, but I don't believe in it being either good luck or
bad luck. I believe in you making it either good or bad
depending on what you do with it. There were some very
negative things that were good luck because of what I did
with it.

I just kept hearing, 'oh, we can't do this because you can't
do this and you can't do this' and I'd spent my whole life
being told that you can't do this and have done it. I know
that if you have a will, there is a way, you know, and
you have to, especially as a woman entrepreneur, you
cannot listen to the Pablum that is passed out.

Part of it is that I did it because they kept telling me I couldn't and I figured, 'Well, you know, what slave ship did you buy me off of?' The worst case is that I'd fail and I'd get another job. So, that's why we are here and so far, so good.

Anytime anyone would say, 'Absolutely not, you won't never be able to estimate a job.' Nobody says 'never' to me. Especially when I'm in control of that deadline. If someone were to say, 'All the money in the world will not be yours,' that would probably be true. But when they say, 'You can't.' I say, 'bull --I can if I want to and I'll decide if I want to or not.' It's very different for somebody to tell me that.

It was not that I was the world's greatest hairdresser or cutter. I had such a huge following that I knew that it was more than my skill that brought those people to me.

The opportunities are there, it's whatever you've got the nerve enough to gamble . . . I am a firm believer that everybody in their lifetime has opportunities to either (a) be successful, (b) make a lot of money, whatever your desire is. If you do not have enough nerve to gamble and take that chance, you're never going to make it. And that's what separates us.

I think my strengths were people skills, dealing with people. I love people. There's not many people who I don't befriend, it is just an attribute, I guess.

I know I am an optimist, I know that I can do it . . . You just know that you can do every single thing you want to do.

I knew it would work. I just always, I think in order to be a successful entrepreneur you have to be sure that it's going to work. If you are not, then you'd better not do it. The whole seminar I attended was on leadership and we did testing before we went that gave you information on the type of person you are. I really got a lot out of that. I learned about myself, but there was really not a lot that I didn't already know. It just confirmed it.

I was different. I got ahead of the rest of the business. The same thing is true in any company, in any business. What makes you better? What makes you be able to make money when everyone else is losing money and closing their doors? We saw foreclosures coming before every other sale in Austin for five years was a foreclosure. I learned what to do with them, how to handle them.

It is important to know that you can run and own a business if you do certain things right. It's reading, applying intuition, applying common sense management. If I didn't know the answer, it was find the answer out.

I mean, up until now, there isn't anything I can't touch that I can't handle. Even though I may not be experienced in it, by God, I'll learn it. So, that's how I feel. That's how confident I am now and have been the rest of the years I've been in this business. Because, I was forced into it. I made this commitment and my parents put their house on the line for me. You think I was going to let them down?

Truly, anything is possible in this life if you really want to work hard enough. There is plenty of work available and plenty of opportunity.

So strong is the sense of self-determination and ability that it influences how these women look at learning. Every day and every experience they had undergone provided a "lesson" or learning.

I always see everything I do as a step up to something else. It is possibility. Things could go in one direction or another. Nothing ventured, nothing gained. Something is bound to pay off someday. The more I learn today, who knows where I will be tomorrow?

Change taught me that I could pull through and that really helped me.

I'm sort of coming to believe that nothing happens by chance. It's all by design. Whatever you see and believe, whether or not it applies to you right now, you stick it into the 15% file you hold in your head of information for future use. Someday you are going to have a need for that. I don't think it comes to you by accident. I think it is by design, some sort of higher design.

I got in my car and was driving home. There was a panel of doctors talking on the radio--you know, nothing happens by accident. They talked about their experience with cancer. The three doctors agreed that the reason why they had been cured was their attitude and positive approach to it. Listening to that, I sat in the car when I got home and I had a long talk with self. I honestly believe that that was the day my whole life turned around.

I refer to it as the luckiest year of my life. I had rheumatic fever, a separation from my husband, a heart block that necessitated a temporary pacemaker, a divorce, and a nervous breakdown all in a nine month period. I learned to delegate. I learned that I had a lot of people who really cared about me, and I learned about my current faith. Between those three things, that's what made that the luckiest year of my life.

I will say I am always, every minute of my working day, every day in my working life, in a consciously learning mode. I feel that if I am observing a business, just about any business has got something that parallels my business, somewhere I can learn what to do, what not to do. I feel that I learn from my customers, I can readily translate things that are appropriate to our business.

The strong internal locus of control did not belie the comments that were made regarding an appreciation for the assistance of God in these women achieving their goals.

I really do feel, and I never start a day without thanking the Lord for what He has given me. With His grace and guidance that we've gotten this far.

Not only do these women have a strong sense of identity, they also hold strong values about life in general. These are fundamental to the how they have fashioned the culture of their organizations. Of primary significance was the value that these women placed on the people who worked with them.

I'm very hands on. I certainly delegate a lot. One of my main assets is having good people and people who have been with me, why, some of them have been with me for fifteen years.

You are only as good as the people you have working for you. I always knew but it took a while to realize that you could pull those strengths out and--what a dynamic group!

One of the biggest concepts in life is fairness, treat people fairly, no matter what they are, no matter what color they are, what sex they are, what religious background they are. You must treat people fairly and you must learn something from every person you meet. I try to live my life that way.

They (the subcontractors) knew I'd be loyal to them and all those guys were with me. Gaining respect had more to do with treating them fairly . . . What matters is, are you fair?

Females are more respected by everyone whether it's male or female just by being yourself and having plain courtesy for individuals.

Some people really care, they really get involved. I've got a few people that really get involved and they really want to do well to the best of their ability and if it takes a little extra, they give a little extra.

Two of the women employ a work force that is primarily unskilled and does manual labor. These women spoke to the many personnel problems they have and their inability to deal effectively with this type of worker. One of these women was Karen Lewis:

> I've got 50 people and every person I hire is another headache. It isn't all wonderful. It's a lot, lot of work. It's frustrating. Because people don't do their job. You can talk to them and they just don't feel like it. Really, really frustrating.

> The man who has the title of supervisor, right now, says it is so busy that he can't watch the other people. I've got another couple of inside sales people. They'll get inquiries. If they answer it, fine, if they don't answer it, fine. That's not right. It's no good for the company.

Marta Garza, who owns a commercial construction business which employs manual and construction trade labor told of how she relates to her employees:

> I get along with Mexican men just fine because I know how to treat them. I learned that from my father. 'Señor, venga por aca. ¿Y porque haces así?' ('Sir, please come here. Why do you do it this way?')

The role of senior executive gives the entrepreneur, of course, the opportunity to practice her beliefs.

> What is right is just basic business principles: do to one as you would have them do unto you. That's what our philosophy is.

> What most people want in their lives is to know that there is something more, something more than what they can see, feel, and touch or that is tangible . . . Something bigger in the universe . . . For me, it is wanting to have the belief that I am God-like, that there is a universal energy that I am.

> We have a real strong motto that if you don't have a good attitude and you don't walk in this office every day with a

good attitude, then you don't work for me. Especially top
management. Because if top management does not have
a positive attitude, you're not going anyplace.

The organizations these women led were characteristically very people-
and family-oriented. Nine of the eighteen entrepreneurs had family
members working in their organizations (even if it was only as a summer
job for a college-aged child). Lil Kohler, a grandmother, employs her son
and daughter as key executives in the company. The day of our interview,
her grandchildren were running and playing in the building, awaiting a
trip with grandma. She started a school for her employees' children as a
way to relieve the stresses associated with day care and to encourage more
family time together.

We are starting a school here, this fall, for our kids,
trying to get the people back together a little bit.

B.T. King, also a grandmother, had her daughter and son-in-law
in key management positions in the company. Her corporate brochure had
pictures of the entire "family" of the company, to include pictures of the
grandchildren and the family pet that doubled as corporate mascot. While
accompanying this president on a tour of the engineering and
manufacturing facility, I was introduced to all the employees, some of
whom had been with the company for more than twenty years. The
president was asked by one of the line workers if his daughter could come
into the facility and wait for the school bus for about a three-week period.
The business owner responded that that would be just fine. In this
particular company, several employees had been employed for over twenty
years.
  Besides setting the tone of the organizational culture, the
entrepreneurs in this study talked about the importance of creating a vision
and sharing it as an integral part of their responsibilities. The women
spoke of sharing their vision and it was linked to learning to meet
challenges. Georgia related a conversation she had had with one of her
subordinates.

He said, 'I could never have the vision you've got; it's one
of the things that has always attracted me to you and has
always made me want to work for you in your business.'
I said that it is hard to convey the vision to somebody
else. It's real hard to hit a moving target. And the vision

is always changing and emerging, it's always growing.
As I learn new things, the vision changes.

Another strong value represented in their organizations was the
emphasis these women placed on developing a company that reflected
quality and doing the job right.

> Quality is part of everything. I learned that years ago.
> Quality starts when you start construction over there and
> it ends when the customer has the product and it works.
> Everything in the middle.

> We are very strong Christian people . . . It's easy to run a
> business if you have a few simple policies or thoughts
> about integrity and fairness and common sense and doing
> what is right. So, we are not out there to gouge the
> companies, we offer a service and that is why we still
> have companies that continue to work with us.

Marta Garza told an anecdote of how she has dealt with a
subcontractor who did not do his best on work he doing for her
construction project. She asked him to remedy the situation and redo his
work.

> The other thing I am known for is that I make them do it
> right because quality is not negotiable. The guy said,
> 'Well, if you want quality, you have to pay me more
> money.' I say, 'No, I don't think so. Where did it say,
> "do it as shitty (sic) as you can and we'll pay you
> anyway." ' Can you imagine? 'Show me where it says
> that and I'll pay you more money!'

The subcontractor redid the work.
Another critical role, which these women spoke of, is one where
they are actively involved with role modeling and training in her
organization. She is an integral part of their learning and connected to
them, sharing what she has learned.

> Nowadays, we draw documents which they (the new
> franchisees) get at various stages, starting them with a
> development manual, a real estate manual advising them
> on how to select their real estate, a concept design kit on

how to build the store, how to lay it out, and everything like that. I had to learn how to do that and it is my responsibility to help them do it the right way.

We did Covey through management and it took a lot of time because I really liked that.

I trained all of our people last fall. Every last person in the company.

That's a great feeling: to educate young people about not squinching when you hear an employee's child at work scream because you were a kid once, too. That's just the way it is. You can be efficient and work around it. You don't have to build a wall, this is home, this is work.

I think my role now is much more like a role I was in this morning. Training people on some of the things I've learned about in the last two days in an Understanding Financial Statements seminar. Informing our people and staying out of their way is a main part of what I do.

We have taken bits of this and bits of that and developed a program that is geared to our people. We've got five managers who teach it. Me, too. They teach it five days a week. We divided our people into groups; in that way, everyone would go through.

In the course of the interviews, the women brought up many of the things they do in the course of carrying out their leadership roles. The women in the study related specific incidents that attested to leadership skills and tasks:

- *strategic planning and forecasting prowess*
In the five-year forecast that I did before I opened the doors, I forecasted $5 million dollars for the fifth year. We did $9 million our third year.

Right now we're at $7.4 million in sales. I see that going to $50 million. Three years ago, our vision was $5 million and we hit that so fast that it wasn't even funny. They were talking at the time maybe $10 million down

the road. If you have a vision and you have a plan . . .
we have a strategic plan, we do have goals, and we do
have a vision of where we want to go and how we want
to be perceived.

- *ability to generate loyalty*
I had a very good reputation when I left Texas
Instruments, not because of what I had done, but because
of the eleven girls I had working behind me. If I went
out at 4:30 in the afternoon and told them that we needed
to ship out 5,000 pieces tonight, all eleven would have
volunteered to stay with me.

- *focus and lead a quality initiative*
I was absolutely astounded last year when I was in
Minneapolis for a quality day when the keynote speaker
got up and spoke about the writing of a quality manual to
start the ISO 9000 process. I can't imagine not having
one--our quality manual, the original one, was written
before we opened our doors.

When we were getting our quality program kicked off, I
went to quality seminars. You reach a point where you
really do not need them anymore. Most of the ones I go
to now, I feel I could teach.

We are still noodling our way through the quality
process. I think it is very difficult for a small company,
particularly one run the way we are with very small
custom jobs on a tight turnaround with slim margins. It
is hard to do something a la Malcolm Baldridge. We
tried it and it just nearly killed us. I am reassessing how
we want to go through the process of improving our
process.

ISO 9000 and the Malcolm Baldridge award, that's
something that I think we'll probably be getting into.
We'll start off with the ISO 9000. No one in our industry
is certified. I want to be the first.

- *defining supplier-customer relationships*
Ours is a high price item, it's not an off the shelf thing
and people are trying to do very complex projects with
our software. We try to treat their initial use of the
software as a joint project. So, we do the work but we
help them plan their use, sort of consultants to them.

- *succession planning*
It is one of my highest priorities. I am in year two of my
five-year plan. What I hope will be a five year deal. I
would like to not be going into work every day in about
three more years.

- *strategic planning and employee involvement*
My group does have a strategic plan. Originally, it was
yearly, but it was too hard to manage. Now we have
quarterly updates. We used to go offsite, and then we
would come back with all the plans that the managers
would try to implement. Wrong. In 1987, we started
training everyone in strategic planning so that anything
we implement would be developed by everyone.

The Learning Process and Resources

How did these women learn how to carry out their leadership
responsibilities? In what kind of learning projects do these women engage
to learn these skills? The learning projects undertaken by the female
entrepreneurs of this study were done so to learn how to solve a business-
related problem or to address a new issue facing her organization for
which the CEO needed to establish a new policy or direction. There
appears to be no formal planning process undertaken to determine what
areas are targets for learning projects. The learning projects are not
"projects" in the sense that they are deliberately planned and carried out.
Instead, the learning falls out of a face-to-face confrontation with the fact
that the woman entrepreneur has to provide an answer to a work-related
problem. She is aware that she knows little about the topic and sets about
to quickly find out as much as she can so she can make an educated
decision.

In the last month and a half, we've learned a lot about importing and exporting. Our bank lost a $35,000 international check. I know how to work those now because I got involved and learned how they flow through the system.

I didn't have time to wait for a serviceman to come, so I insisted on them (the serviceman) teaching me everything. I found out that I was actually quite mechanical, never having known I had any mechanical aptitude whatsoever, because I had never done anything mechanical. I was really very good. I was good at it because I needed to be, because I couldn't afford the down time and I needed to know how to fix the machine myself.

I had not read my first book on franchising. I had no idea of what I was doing (after being approached to enter a franchise arrangement). I called the lawyer the next day to find out what to do. What I found out is that I was already in a pile of trouble! I quickly learned what I needed to do in terms of uniform offering circulars.

Talk to customers and the outside sales people who tell you stuff. In the metal service industry, we have big competition, they are not little guys.

Feedback from others is another way that these women gather information about how well they are doing in the business arena. Sometimes this feedback comes in the form of winning a competition or award. Maria Garcia had been named "Today's Woman" in 1980, "Outstanding Young Woman of America" twice, "Young Career Woman" in 1975 and 1976, and numerous awards for "Business Person of the Year" by the Small Business Administration. Kay Soma commented,

We never entered anything that we haven't won something. Last year was the first year we entered the local Advertising Federation Awards and we took the Best of Show. It was the first year we ever entered. I mean, creatively, we're very strong.

Kay also had numerous statuettes and plaques--awards of appreciation-- on display at her offices that had been given by customers. The importance of customer feedback was reiterated in these comments from other women in the study:

> I think that I take no pleasure other than when we have a problem come up and we solve it or when I see a new, or a new modification go out and we get a letter back from the customer saying how proud they are.

> I was able to give customers what they wanted because I was willing to listen to them, I was willing to change, so I was able to give them what they wanted so I kept growing and growing and growing and growing.

The feedback may have even been something as simple as

> When I gave the commencement speech at her school a couple of years ago at Christmas, a little woman had a newspaper clipping in her pocketbook. She said that she had saved it about me two years ago and she had always wanted to meet me.

This continued cycle of feedback and reinforcement for what they were doing, again, replicates the feedback and support these women had experienced since their youth and again, reinforces the concept that these women did not operate or learn in isolation.

These women continue the pattern of learning that relied on interactions with others when they utilized the compensated assistance of a subject matter expert. Hiring someone to help provide needed information could be more expedient than setting about to research, learn, and master that specialized area herself.

> If you don't know how to do something, hire someone else to do it. I mean, there are things when you need a CPA or you need an attorney, whatever, so you pay your money and take your hour.

> Then you have the professionals who you pay by the hour to train you.

> We're, um, through our involvement with total quality management, we have one of these talks every six weeks. We send people to facilitation workshops, and then the guy comes over every six weeks and we're doing communication skills and he's helping us develop all our systems and everything like that.

A significant professional for Belinda Watkins, who sued the city to fight for fairness in contracting was her attorney.

> I went to lawyers and, God bless his soul, I will always, always owe 'Bob Taylor' a piece of my soul, because most lawyers wouldn't take it. And Bob took the suit. He decided to help me fight the establishment.

Sometimes the person who the entrepreneur relies on is hired into the organization to provide a continued source of learning and support for the business owner. Cammy Hargrove talked about how she had hired a "good old boy," a man who could do marketing and networking in her industry, one which is primarily male-dominated . She had learned that

> they're very polite to me but they don't trust me, they don't want to play golf with me, and they don't want to be my friend. So, I need to provide someone that can do that. I guess that's just a reality of doing business in this particular industry.

Her response was to adapt to a problem by hiring someone whom could meet a need for her. However, the person who she had originally hired was lured away by the competition, a firm started by another former employee. She was on the verge of hiring a new "right hand man." Georgia recounted a more positive experience:

> Finding products was one of the big challenges. I then went about learning. I brought someone in from the very beginning, a long-term friend of mine, who was a registered massage therapist. He had a lot of anatomical knowledge that I was totally lacking. He taught me a lot about the back side of it and I taught him a lot about business, about selling. He's now one of the vice-presidents of the company.

B.T. King relied on the head of her engineering department to teach her about the hands-on technical parts of the business, with much success. She defines her organization as a "family."

Among the women in the study, only four discussed someone in their organization as a business associate who provided support and assistance. They were people who they had met and known in previous environments:

> Joanne Jones, who went to work with me the same year I went to work at TI, 1960 is in sales here. When I went to work at Company T, I called her and asked her if she would come out to help me. She did. She was my right arm.

> He was helping his dad build Circle K's at the time I first hired him. We used to live in the same mobile home park and we got in this bowling league together. We became friends, his wife and I and him. And then, his dad got cut off from building Circle K's and so he found himself out of a job . . . Now of all the employees, he's still with me. He's been with me 17 years. He's a vice president of the company now.

Building these relationships was not always easy for the entrepreneur. Kate Hammond, the owner of the high tech software company said:

> It took me a while to figure out whether to trust her (her partner) and then took her a little while to see if she could trust me. The thing that is really nice about the relationship is that we do have a lot of trust. It's real important. She is sales and marketing.

Several of the women in this study had spouses who had corporate business experience; these women routinely relied on their husbands for advice, support and encouragement:

> Weekends, advice, suggestions, good advice on management style. Some of this is around how I want to be treated, so how would I treat other employees? It's usually, because he's been in management, that's where I've learned the most. He asks me 'Have you thought

about this, where did this come from?' So I've really
learned a lot and bounced a lot off him.

My husband would talk things over with me, we'd talk
about ceramics not being conductive and could it be used
in position? It would be bad because it could crack and
heat could flow on it and this, that, and the other . . . A
lot of it come about over the dinner table.

My husband, being more of a management type, has
always told me, 'if you have to answer right now, the
answer is "no." If you have time to digest it and look at
it, think about it, and see what all the possibilities are,
then maybe.' I don't think I answer when people hit me
with questions that don't have a 'yes, no, black, white'
answer as quickly.

My husband has said many, many times, 'Paula, I've
never known you to take on a project where you didn't do
your best, didn't know how to do what you set out to do.'

My husband, Bob, has more warrior background. He's
just a real savvy people person. He has a sound business
background.

I use him (my spouse) and my son . . . I get the
impression that he doesn't want a blow by blow of my
day and I don't want to spend my time giving him one.
There are other things I'd rather be doing but if I had a
decision that I have been wrestling over, and because I
have been, or I can't seem to pull all the pieces together
from a disparate point of view, then I will talk to him
about it. He is very smart and his critical thinking skills
are different from mine so I feel I have some . . . he is
not involved in the company except as an advisor.

I've got my best friend. My husband loves me and
understands and complements me so I do get my boosts!
A lot of friends at my age are facing mid-life crises, have
raised their children and are having husbands who are
divorcing them. So, I have a lot to be thankful for. Jim
helps me to see different perspectives. When I'm wrong

or I need to understand, he's always been very good at seeing the other side. He helps me look at things from one side and another.

It's nice to have reached the point where I no longer need him to be involved in the business decision. Does that make sense? I wouldn't be here if it weren't for him encouraging me to do this, I would never have thought of this. We have just grown and grown and grown.

Dana Johnson, the head of the full service real estate business worked very closely with her husband: together they owned six companies that were interrelated. They strength of their business relationship reinforced her sense of confidence. She explained it this way:

My husband and I got married when we were 28. He was a really good friend; I had done a lot of business with him. I am eight months older than he is, he has a law degree . . . decided he didn't want to practice law, he wanted to build. So he did all the Trammell Crow shopping centers at 22, 23. So, in our getting married at 28, I had my company and he had his and there are about six corporations now that all complement each other. If Austin isn't doing something that I can make money in, then Rick and I will shoot out to wherever and we will be doing an office building wherever. Because we have all the demographics, our commercial entity gave us the foundation to be able to do anything we want all over this world, actually.

For some entrepreneurs, the interviews identified another trend that of the female business owner routinely turning to associates in the same industry. This uncompensated guidance is based upon personal relationships:

I think any owner needs to get involved with their industry. I sit on the state board, I've been a state past president, I've been a local past president, so I've got mentors around the state that have been in business twenty years. I can pick up the phone and call 'Harry' in Houston and say, 'Harry, I've got a problem. I need some advice, can I come and talk to you?' He's so successful and always will help.

I've been very active in a national level of a quick printing association. It's a huge network of friends across the country. I can ask questions very specific to my business, but if I need an answer from someone else, I can call any number of associates around the country. 'What are you spending on this?' We are not in competition, since we live in different cities.

The source of the uncompensated guidance may come from a mentor who is an investor. Kate Hammond told of two investors to her business:

We had only two investors . . . one of them is a wonderful person. He's a personal investor. 'John Smith' who had been a founder of MCC and he was actually a great asset during this time. 'Bob Jones' is an investor to our Board. And, I've gone to John with more sort of open-ended questions than to Bob. About how do I make the transition, when I make the transition? You know, how do I grow the company? Those guys, they've been around, they are very valuable, they've done a lot. John on a couple of occasions has given me good advice on how to succeed.

The personal investor of whom this entrepreneur spoke had assisted her by persuading another investor to allow the entrepreneur "some more time" to be able to pull the company out of a rough period. It was a funding-related problem related to timing and accounts receivables; she did pull the situation together with time.

Being a member of an association or a board for a civic association or community group also provided learning assistance to these women:

I belong to the National Association of Women Business Owners, so you kind of compared notes there about what was happening.

A lot of the training that I can use for my own business has been acquired by belonging on the Boards because they, like anyone else, they discuss financials, they discuss plans of action, they discuss strategic planning . . . and so I've learned a lot by belonging on the Boards.

I bring that back and can apply it in some form or fashion here. That's helped a great deal. That's probably the best education I've ever gotten is belonging on the Boards.

We have conferences yearly, we have a local association and each of the, most of the bigger cities have local associations. We bring speakers and industry trainers in and we share those with the other local associations, so many of the people who have been in the business. Like the gentleman I referred to who has been in the business for twenty years, he would come to our association and didn't charge us a penny and did our installation and talked about what he sees for the future. There are industry trainers, so it's education, it's watching the legislation.

I certainly learned a lot by serving on volunteer boards. I think that that is a very good way to learn about how things are done. And that's another networking opportunity where you can make friends.

I have attended a lot of seminars and what has really helped me is being out in the business world and being with business people. I have since joined the Executive Committee which is a group of company presidents or owners of companies and there is not two in the group the same and they act as your Board of Directors. You bring them your problem, they discuss it, they'll tell you what's good or bad about it, and they give you a lot of suggestions. It's been really good.

Some of the organizations that I belong to, have given me access to business people. My phone bill gets real high.

Of course, we participate with the Women's Chamber of Commerce, the Women's Business Center, and the Women in Construction group.

Associations are not the answer to all women in business, however. Ann Mills expressed disappointment in having been a member of the National Association of Women Business Owners but felt that those meetings were

> so calculated. All it is passing business cards. Women thinking that they are going to get business from other women.

On those rare occasions where the female entrepreneurs in this study did engage in a learning project that was planned, it was associated with becoming certified through a formal organization for credentialling. Paula talked about such a process in her industry:

> For new people coming into the business, they can go through this program called 'Teach.' It's a self-taught thing and you take a test when you are done. Once you've been in the business, then you can take the Certified Personnel Consultant test. You have to go to San Antonio, there is a proctor there. It is a national test and you have a part on the law and the legal aspects of the business. I have done it and all but one of my staff members has.

The importance of learning with others and staying connected with is evident in any planned learning projects as well. Personal affiliations are regarded a way to continue to grow and to learn. Ann Mills put it this way:

> Going back to get the MBA had very little to do with the functional information that I was going to get from that program. Everybody was working full-time. We had Billy Clayton, who was ex-Speaker of the House, we had a guy who was a physician and also an attorney, who was going back for his MBA. We had Rob Germao, whose father was Joe Germao, who fought the Pennzoil case, someone else who used to be deputy health commissioner. Just amazing people in the program. So that really suited my purposes. I met some dynamic people that I learned from.
>
> Small business is very isolating. There are no built in mentors. People in large organizations have somebody

they respect who they can watch that is obviously more
skilled than they are in the profession, they can watch
and learn. I don't. The people you have are other peers
who are in similar industries, but it takes a lot more
energy to go out and find and then observe those people.

Caren Thomas, who relied extensively on the networks she had
established not only in her business but also in her role as the chair of the
Chamber of Commerce, recognized the importance of relationships in
receiving assistance and assisting others as an exchange process.

Relationships are key . . . it's like, what you do for others
and what they do for you. It all works. There are a lot of
takers, who just want you to do for them and then they
don't reciprocate. Or they ask you for advice and don't
do anything with the advice and then come back again.

The role of seminars in development is not widely used by the
women interviewed in the study. Cost of external seminars as well as the
basic level of information provided in public seminars was given as
reasons for non-attendance. When they are attended, the seminars are
specialized and, again, business-related.

We go to a variety of things. I get maybe ten or fifteen
different things across my desk every morning. We
belong to the local Human Resources association.
Eileen (her HR director) belongs to that and I belong to
it. So Eileen is pretty good about going to those
seminars . . . Legal firms have been very good about
putting on some lunchtime seminars and I try to go to
those.

We started roasting our own coffee, so I went to a
coffee seminar last year in Seattle and accumulated
information to try to make decisions. We were serving
cappuccino but then we decided to roast our own
because we make our own ice cream and we are
defining what differentiates us even from excellent
companies like Starbucks. We've done a lot of research
and put together print materials to educate our
consumers.

The personal development work I did actually led me to
the thoughts that we are doing more than cutting a head
of hair. The first work that I really did that made a huge
impact was Werner Erhardt's work.   It was like
snatching your face away from the wall.   I had taken
some regular classes and seminars offered in local hotels.
I realized one day that this was not it . . . Once I did the
work with my energy, I knew I would never go back to
sit down seminars . . . there was never a lot of
spirituality. What I am doing now is incorporating the
energy training with the quality training.

The only real organized seminar I'd been to was the
very first Inc. Women in Business. I was appalled.
Then, I'm scared because I can't spend $800 easily, and
then there is travel.

Who has time?

I do attend conferences. Usually they are the same,
they get repetitious, kind of general reminder that that
is what you need to do.

Despite the predominant perspective that formal schooling did not and
does not provide the necessary skills for these women to own and lead their
businesses, Paula who talked about returning to school to complete her
degree expressed the value of education.

Education is important. I've thought of going back to St.
Ed's and finishing my degree because they do have a
program where you can apply your life experiences. But
not now. Later, when I have time and I'm tired of doing
this.

Georgia Roberts had, indeed, completed her degree through the program at
St. Edward's University and did apply her life experiences--after she had
become a millionairess.   Maria Garcia also talked about her desire to
return to school.

What I wanted to do was go back to college and get right
to the meat of it, you know? I didn't want to have to
worry about English, it bored me, is really what

happened. Now, I regret it, today, because had I done it then, I think I'd be much better off. Obviously, it's like anything else. If you have the proper training in certain areas then the chances of your succeeding or not making it though the mistakes are greater. So, I regret it today, not having been able to go back and have that four-year degree.

Individual reading of books, journals, and magazines were also cited as ways to acquire information to stay informed on business-related issues. On many of the desks I saw in offices, there were journals (a couple of *Harvard Business Reviews*, trade periodicals, news periodicals.) To a lesser degree did I observe bookshelves with current and popular books. Books that I did see were a two or three topical management books and many more technical books (i.e. software language, company-related loose-leaf binders). Maria Garcia was an exception in her avid interest in reading.

Anything that has to do with accounting manuals, in my case, I get the flyers and the newspapers from the CPA firms that used to do my accounting. For all the updates. I love to read all of it. It's the kind of reading I enjoy. But, for pleasure reading, it is science fiction.

Lisa Bollcher remarked,

I'm an avid reader, too, that helps. I don't get to read as much as I mean to, periodicals.

To a far lesser extent do they engage in learning for a hobby or non-work related area. Although most of the learning of this group of women was work-related, there was some discussion of the non-business related learning activities, which are pursued for relaxation, interest, and hobbies.

I am addressing myself in my personal life to try to spend more time developing my skills in non-business areas. I heard about this Old Time American music and I just thought it was the greatest thing I ever heard . . . It is happy, it's jolly, it's clear, it's uncomplicated, and I want to be able to make that kind of music. So, I set about learning it. I am also taking singing

lessons because I have always sung. I realized
some time ago that I would probably be a lot
better if I had lessons. So, I've been doing that
and I really enjoy it.

About four years ago, I took up horseback riding.
It was something I always wanted to do ever since
I was a kid, but it was one of those things that
when you're a kid and you say, 'Oh, I want a
horse and I want to learn how to ride,' and your
parents go, 'yeah, yeah, yeah. . .where are we
going to put this thing? We'll get that right after
we get the motorcycle and the spaceship, you
know?' And so, I woke up one day, I was 36 years
old and I said, 'Why not learn how to ride a horse
this year?' So I got in my station wagon and drove
out on IH-10 and pulled into the thing that said,
'Riding Lessons' and said that I wanted to start
taking riding lessons.

Ann Mills had been a marathon runner but due to back problems picked a
new sport that would be less stressful to her back--professional women's
boxing.

It is a thinking sport. The movement, the
response, the energy--it's probably the most
thinking sport I've ever done. I got into it because
I love sports.

Sports and physical exercise was also the direction that Caren Thomas
took:

When I chaired the Chamber that year, 95 companies
visited Austin to talk about relocating and, indeed, 25
did. We were 7th in the nation that year with new job
creation. I went to 95 dinners and gained 20 pounds.
Then, I went to the Metropolitan Club over there . . . and
I hired a personal trainer. I had never done anything like
that in my life. Now it has really become addictive . . .
At least six days out of seven, I walk four miles in the
morning, I do the treadmill for an hour at night, plus I
use weights until I can bench-press 65 pounds.

Belinda Watkins took training in the Fire Department and volunteers as a fire fighter.

> It was a great experience for anyone to learn--requires teambuilding skills.

The Continual Process of Learning

The female entrepreneurs in this study recognized that a continual process of learning and adapting to change was essential. It is a natural extension of what they have been doing all their lives.

> In this industry (real estate), you must know that you will have continual challenge and be adaptive.

> That helps, to know that you can like, redefine yourself, which we are all going to have to do more of in the future. Right? Just because of the rate of change. I'm still learning! Again, a lot of the things that you need to know in business is common sense. And just plain downright common courtesy, loyalty, and trust.

> I think that there are even more things that I want to know about now than I did when I was growing up. I have wider ranging interests and I have an awareness of what a friend calls my 'islands of ignorance.' I guess I am more aware of them and why it is important that they become smaller islands. I have to say that I had continents of ignorance and not just islands! The more I learn, the more I realize there are things I want to learn about.

> I sort of feel that I'm on the brink of something, I don't know exactly what it is or what form it will take but, I know that it is going to be different. I'm trying to open my mind and get ready for it, whatever it is. One of these days, it is going to appear.

Continued learning includes keeping watch on the types of developments that will affect the success of their businesses. This challenge of staying competitive and keeping the customers satisfied is very much the focus of business-oriented learning for these women.

> We've got 25 customers. Our tools sell from anywhere from one quarter of a million to $300,000 and we are selling to people who have pain, in spades. You can support 25 to 30, 35 people, paper, good will, and lots of hard work but when you start going into 200, you better have your processes in place, you'd better have your systems in place. Because people get real intolerant if they give you a quarter of a million and you don't ship them stuff on time. So that is our challenge now to get those sort of mechanisms in place and keep within our cost. And, next year, it will be something else.

Plans for the future include starting new businesses; success at building one business is translated to positive thoughts about doing it again.

> I just want to keep growing. Really, that was one of the reasons we went into the air conditioning business. If air conditioning goes, what I'm hoping is in two years, I'm going to start another branch. Something else.

> Well, there are a couple of business ideas that I have that I wouldn't have to be in on every day after I got somebody (to take over her duties). And, I would love to write.

> It is sort of liberating from that point of view, having done it once.

Goals for the future and learning new things often include spending more time with others. Recognition of the need for balance in one's life is evident in their thinking.

> There are lots of other things I'd like to do, um, I have a husband who is wonderful who is twelve years older than I am and life is short. And, this is a sixty, seventy hour a week business, there should be a time for more balance in my life. That's my long-term goal. Like, I want to take sculpting. I want to do other things.

There are other parts of life that would be nice in addition . . . there's a book I'd like to write someday and stuff like that. But I've got to get this little baby to a certain point and then move on.

Throughout their lives, their learning has been intertwined with other people. This being connected to someone who can be a role model or mentor is exemplified in these statements:

Where, how do you mentor up at Austin, Texas? I can call anyone and get them to return the call, but how do I grow? How do you grow yourself? So, there really have to be some people I think out of town and where do I go for the next step? I'm giving that some thought now.

You never get too old to learn. Your problem is finding the people you want to teach you.

Eliza Brady talked about the importance of networking, another way of utilizing relationships and alliances with other people, to assist in her learning.

I learn experientially and I learn by listening to other people and I have learned, as a lot of people have, that networking, which is just making friends, it gets you in front of a database of friends, of people who are willing to talk to you. You do have to be thoughtful about where you spend your time.

Sharing Their Knowledge and Learnings With Others

Again and again, the women in this study talked about how they are contributing to the development of others. These women felt an obligation, a responsibility in sharing the information and learning they have acquired with others. They wanted to make a difference in the lives of others.

It's really exciting when I see, and I think that's part of the reason of why I love this business, when you're making a difference in somebody's life. You're providing an opportunity (through placing the person on a job).

> They're going out there and doing it all; they're shining
> like a star and then they are being offered a job.

> I also think that for those of us who are leaders really
> need to think about what you are going to do to improve
> Austin in 1994, what are you going to do to improve
> Texas in 1994, what you are going to do to improve the
> country or what are you going to do to improve the
> world?

There were two primary areas that are outlets for this sharing.
One was with other women and the other was with the community in
general.

Part of the desire to share their knowledge and learnings with
other women was to provide other women with the benefit of their
experiences.

> You know, they need, we need to make sure that these
> women are moving up faster than all of us did to get
> there. I am concerned these days about backslides . . .
> When I speak to the graduate school of business at UT,
> those women, I really want to tell them in an hour, an
> hour and a half, every challenge that I have had, every
> pitfall to make them aware but also to get them there
> faster.

> I spend a lot of time now mentoring. Women my own
> age, younger women. Right now I have a group of
> women, about twenty of them, that I have kept in my
> Daytimer. You know, I'd have a meeting at Dell or at
> Apple and I'd notice that a woman was really sharp. So,
> then in the summer, I had a meeting at my house and I
> said, 'You all come and then you can decide what you
> want to do from them on.' They range in age from like
> 22 to 35, and they meet now once a month, and then I
> give them resources, and they have had had some, really
> . . . everybody in this town is available to speak.

Belinda Watkins chaired a small business development initiative
to help provide business-related information for women. The message she
shares with businesswomen is:

The other thing that I really preach to successful women is that you have got to reach your hands back and pull someone else up. If you think that you are secure in your position, you are out of your G-- damned mind . . . The up side of that is that females are now in a unique opportunity, never seen before in the economic history of America. They can dictate entirely new ways of doing things.

This sharing with women is not just focused on grown females: Cammy Hargrove described her sharing project as follows.

I am a grown up Girl Scout. I am a member of the Mirrors project, which is adult mentoring for the girls. I am also a member of the Board; this is my second time around. So, we try to do, my sister and my daughter both are Girl Scouts, so we try and help. It's a wonderful program. Almost all the girls that I know who have stayed with scouting have emerged to be the leaders of their generation. I find that extremely significant.

Caren Thomas chaired the city Chamber of Commerce and found it was an opportunity to create opportunities for women as well as serve her community.

When I chaired the Chamber . . . we had eight people of the board when I started and how one third are women. That was a big success for me, bringing in very strong women. It is not enough just to be there, you have to make yourself known.

This woman perceived her involvement with the Chamber as an on-going way to influence other businesses and organizations.

That was high visibility and still is, because you find out after you chair the Chamber that that is a position that so few people have in a community that you get automatically called upon for multiple boards, multiple experiences, multiple speeches.

The value of serving on boards was important to this entrepreneur. Caren viewed them as vehicles for change--that of introducing the influence of women.

> I'm addicted to work. You really have to decide, like some strong boards I'm asked to be on, that I think are strong boards, you can't say 'no.' Then they'll say, 'We asked Caren Thomas and she turned us down.' Now that (serving on them) will exhaust you, so now I have to say, 'No, but someone else who has the same skills that I do, have you thought of them?'

Sharing with the community took many forms. For some women, it meant serving on community boards that are desired to assist the disadvantaged or minority groups. Kay Soma said:

> I serve on some boards. I'm on the board of the Funding Information Center. Um, I recently went on the executive board of the Boy Scouts, I'm the Chairman for Handicapped Scouting, so yeah, that's gonna be really neat. And then, I'm on the Board of the San Antonio Educational Partnership, which is the board that Henry Cisneros started to help kids in traditionally high dropout schools. They have to make at least a B-average and 95% attendance and they are guaranteed a financial aid package or preference for a good job when they get out of school. And, one of my clients, last year gave a $300,000 gift to the partnership so that was really neat. And, then a couple of advisory boards where I don't have to go to the meetings, I just have to give people advice, which is my favorite thing to do! 'Cause I don't have a lot of time to go to meetings, so I miss quite a few.

Paula Goodman had this to say about her community involvement:

> I feel like we have to give back to the community and that's another thing our organization does. We are real active in our chamber board, American Red Cross. My recruiters have freed me up, a blessing to me because it also allows us to build credibility in our industry.

The two women who were of Hispanic heritage were active in Mexican American associations and felt a responsibility to contribute their learnings in this area.

> I've learned so much that I'm doing consulting in minority participation as they relate to ordinances. I would be there to help the people get through the ordinances. Expanding into something else because I know the ordinances. I know from the minority point of view what has to be done . . . This is a payback and pulling people up, reaching out and helping a lot of my people. If I can get in, they can get in.

> I've gotten involved in the community since several years back but I belong to the Mexican American Unity Council. I'm on the Board, I'm a vice chairman there, and, of course, it is a non-profit organization and they do a lot of services for the community, alcohol prevention, that kind of thing. I belong to the Goodwill Industries Board for many years, I'm sure you've heard of them. I belong to the Bexar County Medical Board, just a lot of community work.

There were many evidences of this community involvement on the office walls of the women who met with me in their corporate headquarters. I had many opportunities to observe plaques and certificates of appreciation from varied community and business associations. Often, an accompanying photograph of the entrepreneur and a community leader was present on the wall as well.

Another avenue of sharing and reaching out for some of the women was an articulated involvement with their church.

> We are both active in our church, we both teach, he drives the bus and we do like that portion of our life. We get our energy doing it. We sing in our choir, too.

> I was doing volunteer work at the B'hai faith in areas of socio-economical development primarily in third world countries. I was loving what I was doing.

Because two of the women had been recognized in the community for their contributions in the area of quality, they felt they could provide the most assistance in this area. One of these women, Beth Cole Milne, was developing a proposal to submit to a college Quality awareness program in application for an adjunct position for she felt she had significant experience in instituting total quality management in a small business and could share that with others. The other woman, Lil Kohler, felt that by extending invitations to inquiring businesses, she could contribute to their development.

> If anyone comes in, we'll help them with quality information. We still make sure the little guy gets the quality attitude installed and make them aware.

The oldest woman in the interviewed group, B.T. King, contributed to sponsoring young people through the 4H. She paid over $20,000 of her personal funds to buy a steer that had been raised by a young man, and then provided him with part-time after school employment.

> That $20,000 secures his education.

Making a difference, contributing overall to the betterment of society, and feeling good that they are doing something was a theme I heard again and again from these women in the study. They believe in giving back some of what they have been able to take.

> I ended up in the ice cream business when I was going to med school because it is so enticing. It is a wonderful place to be. People are so happy when they eat ice cream . . . Our lives are getting rougher and rougher and rougher and there are fewer and fewer breaks in our day. Ice cream is just this panacea product to sell.

> Our whole goal for the company is working with the community and really playing a positive, significant role in the community is very important to us.

> I think the world really needs to be humanized. It is not a masculine or feminine thing. It's a human thing. I think the time is right.

V

Discussion of Findings, Conclusions, and Implications of this Study

DISCUSSION OF FINDINGS

This exploratory study used a naturalistic, descriptive approach to examine the nature of learning as it exists in the life of eighteen Central Texas women entrepreneurs. Following the constructs for a study employing a naturalistic paradigm, the study did not test specific hypotheses, but sought to develop understanding of adult learning as it exists for the subject group as described by the participants in the study. This work was guided by the proposition that adults do engage in learning as a natural and on-going process in their lives. The findings of this research explored what and how a group of successful women learn. The study identified the patterns of learning and the importance of learning as an integral part of the lives of this select group.

An integral part of this research was the use of the women's words--their voices--to describe learning in their lives. The antecedents for this particular approach lie in the philosophical foundations of feminist research. Carol Gilligan's *In a Different Voice* (1982) describes women's development in the context that the way that people talk about their lives is of significance, that the language that they use and the connections they make reveal the world that they see and in which they see. This context, then, frames the findings that emerged from the interviews with the women of this study. Each woman interviewed talked about her life and her development using her own "voice" to describe significance and meaning. Each one talked about the panorama of her life as an education, supporting Lindeman's contention that "if education is life, then life is education" (1926). The content of the data further supported the Rogerian tenets that learning has a personal involvement, is pervasive, is evaluated by the learner, and its essence is meaning (Rogers, 1961).

RESEARCH QUESTIONS

The research questions guiding this research were:

1. What do female entrepreneurs learn and why?
2. How do they learn? How is this demonstrated?
   What methods or processes do they use?
3. What resources do they rely upon in their learning
   endeavors?
4. How do they describe their learning?
5. What factors affect their learning?

A discussion of each of these questions and associated interview findings follows.

Research Question 1: What do female entrepreneurs learn and why?

The women in this study described learnings in two primary areas: to continually define their sense of self and to solve business-related problems by gaining information that helps them to lead and operate their businesses.

The process of defining themselves started in their childhoods. Their childhoods were full of experiences, which developed a strong sense of who they were, a strong values and belief orientation, and a strong interest in business-related activities. These experiences provided the foundation for who they are today; the "starting point" for their moral development and sense of self (Gilligan, 1982). Sixteen of the women in this study were in the leadership cohort of the "Instigators" which Astin and Leland identified, women in their forties and early fifties whose families allowed them to develop as independent women with strong beliefs in social justice and the work ethic (1991). They acquired many of the values of their parents at the same time that they were gathering self-confidence and an appreciation of their own selves.

As these women grew into maturity, their self-images continued to develop and they learned they could overcome adversity. Most were able to gain one job after another; a skill especially useful as these women often needed to support themselves and their children. They had learned that they possessed the personal abilities to overcome whatever difficulties came their way.   They were willing to work at any type of job and were willing to do just about anything in order to keep their families solvent. Two women lied in order to get a job; rather than suffer any negative consequences, they used those jobs as stepping-stones to better positions. The ability to handle problems or challenges further enhanced these women's self-images. Lombardo's premise that a self-fulfilling prophecy approach of success in management breeds more success (1982) is evident as these women gained more self-confidence with each success they achieved.

While employed by others, the women were provided opportunities in the work place to grow. Whether it was learning "at the expense of others" who had fiscal and overall responsibility, or whether it was learning in an organizational setting under a mentor's tutelage, these women were not satisfied with remaining static. There was a picture of wanting to learn because it was viewed that this was how to "move ahead." It may have not been clear exactly what the goal or target specifically looked like, however, the women were often convinced that things could be done better. Moreover, they believed that <u>they</u> could do it better. They believed that had the power to change their lives and survive.

The women in this study described how, while they were working for others, they acquired skills which would help them when they started their own businesses. One woman was the first woman manager at a Fortune 500 technical company and turned her group into the most profitable group in that company. Another had several experiences in startup operations and all the tasks that initiation of a new business venture requires--and the importance of bringing people with potential and aptitude to work in the organization. The women spoke, not only of positive work experiences, but also negative practices, which they would not utilize when they were in charge. Overall, they learned how to get the job done by and with other people's help.

Almost every experience the women spoke of involved some learning for them. For example, the decision to start their own businesses was often unpremeditated. Several of the women described an opportunity that had presented itself, and, since they had learned self-efficacy in the past, they took advantage of the situation and "jumped in," sure that they would make it work. It didn't matter that perhaps they didn't have the capital or have a location or have the corporate details in place. Those were obstacles that could easily be overcome. Obstacles in their past had been overcome by personal attitude and determination and the problems associated with business startup would not get in the way. Each new situation taught them they could succeed.

Once the decision had been made to start the business, the women described learning the things they needed to do to keep the doors open and be profitable. Writing business plans, developing customers, securing the services of attorneys and CPAs were among some of the tasks that the women knew they needed to learn. These women described learning how to solve a business-related problem, fitting Knowles' description of a problem-oriented adult learner (1975). This is the learner who comes into an educational activity largely because she is experiencing some inadequacy or lack of knowledge in dealing with a real-life problem. In the course of everyday activity, an issue arose (like franchising or an accounting problem) and the woman needed to get an answer immediately. Spontaneity and the need for a "just-in-time" response characterize the situation. This, too, supports Knowles' belief that the time perspective is critical due to the need for application of learning. These women are like Knowles' model of self-directed learner in that they decide what they need to learn and when.

Like other business owners, these women are concerned with ensuring the continued success of their businesses. For some, future plans include selling the business and trying a new endeavor, for others, continuing to grow their current enterprise. For three of the eighteen women, the thinking about the future included developing formal plans to leave their business at fifty (barring no unforeseen crisis) and engage in some other business practice. This entails learning and exploring their options. These women closely fit the Houle (1961) typology of a goal-oriented learner who is learning for goal accomplishment. This was a minority approach to thinking about the future, however. For the rest of the women, there was an almost "wait and see" approach, with very little described planning of what the next few years will bring. Almost every woman talked about engaging in strategic planning. Those with children in their business were concerned about how they might transition the business to the children's control. One woman described difficulties with the lack of initiative demonstrated by the inheriting children and her perception that they lacked the interest or the motivation to succeed in the business she has worked so hard to develop. She indicated that she would probably sell the business. She definitely wanted to start another business and just needed to "have the right moment appear."

Only a handful of the women in this study discussed learning something non-business-related to provide balance in their lives. One woman personified Houle's learning activity model (1961): she wanted to learn horseback riding since childhood and now that she has become a prosperous businesswoman and can afford it, she bought a horse. She had to consciously map out and plan a training program to learn how to ride this horse. Another had recently retained a personal trainer to focus on her physical health. She walks four miles each morning and works out in a gym, something she has to be deliberate about in scheduling. Both of these women described learning projects and activities that were deliberate, intentional, and planned, like those described by Tough (1967).

Research Question 2: How do they learn? How is this demonstrated? What methods or processes do they use?

Whether the women in this study talked about how their childhood experiences shaped their self-images or about the learnings they acquired through previous employment or in their business startup, they talked about their relationships with others, connected through their experiences with significant others.

In childhood, they acquired a sense of importance by going somewhere with mom or dad or by being the only one dad asked to help out with a work project. They knew they were special as parental attention was provided to the child who accompanied her father as he delivered lumber, who attended a university class with her mother, or whose father arranged that she summer on ships in the port of Houston.

The women talked about how they came to believe that they were different from their siblings and peers, again, comparing themselves with others because they like to do certain things and others didn't or they could excel at some unusual activity.

The women described how their images of themselves were formed as they were rewarded and reinforced by those closest to them in their lives. All but two of the women described their childhoods in families where they were supported and encouraged to do their best. That these to-be leaders had family supporting relationships is in line with the findings of Baraka-Love (1986) and Goldwasser (1988) which suggest that successful women leaders have family supporting relationships which reinforce their feelings of competency. They described relationships with their mothers, their fathers, or another persons who made an impact on their life and from whom they learned about themselves. Their mothers and fathers had voices which articulated values such as integrity, respect for others, and caring. The remembrances that the women had of these people were positive, encouraging, and, usually demonstrative of emotion and caring. The familial influences of the women in this study were much like the family life attributes of the Constructivists of Belenky, Clinchy, Goldberger, and Tarule (1986).

It is interesting that the women in this study did not talk about any school-type experiences or relationships with teachers as role models or mentors to them at young ages. The sense one gets from these women is that it was a lot more fun making money or doing "grown up" things than playing with dolls or being in clubs at school. School was not important or a source of inspiration for these women.

In their young adulthood, the way the women in this study learned was through a variety of experiences that often included the involvement of others. In their employment experience of working for others, they continued to learn more about themselves, their capabilities and strengths. This finding was supportive of the research of Van Velsor and Hughes (1990). They had jobs like running a day care center for younger children, working as a nurse on Indian reservations, waitressing and then working as a manager in a series of restaurants, working as a teacher's aide, teaching linguistics in a university, working for a Boy Scout Explorer council, and managing a small bank where customer service included reconciling customer's checking accounts. Other jobs included working as a bookkeeper, selling real estate, serving as a bartender in a military officer's club, working as an architect's office manager, renovating homes and managing a commercial builder's office, and employment as a legal assistant. Whether she was learning how to deal with difficult people (in a bar), or negotiating with subcontractors over price (while renovating a house) or learning how to coach a sales team (as a commercial realtor), each of these women described how she learned how to deal with people interpersonally and prove herself successful and capable.

The women participants of this study learned by their experiences. This is consistent with the constructs developed by Lindeman (1926) and Rogers (1961). The richness of the learning they derived from their experiences, the life-centered nature of their learning, and the how they can reflect on the significance of what they have experienced are congruent with the theoretical framework of adult learning.

Research Question 3: What resources do they rely upon in their learning endeavors?

In all their prior work experiences, the women spoke of working with other people. It is interesting that several of the women in this study described having developed long-lasting relationships with former fellow employees or former employers, some of whom they would rely on when the women started their own businesses. These relationships were built on mutual respect and trust: based on the woman's ability to do a good job and be a dependable, competent employee. On the other side of the exchange, the women recognized early on that they could learn from other people, that they could benefit by the relationship, and that others could help them-

-they only needed to ask. Some of these people were to be mentors and role models, from whom these women received business-related or technical information as well as morale support. The strength of these relationships is evident in the fact that some of these mentors supplied monetary support to their protégés as well as long-term counsel across many miles.

Like the self-directed learners which Penland described in his survey of self-directed learners (1979), the women interviewed here sought assistance in the start up phase from a dependable resource base: friends, spouse, and close business associates. Long-time mentors and business associates were invaluable in providing support and encouragement, as well as being able to answer questions that needed answering. A spouse with business experience was often the person to whom the female entrepreneur turned for guidance on process and procedure. The spouse did not directly work for the entrepreneur but, rather, served as a shadow consultant behind the scenes. This corresponds to the findings of Neider (1987) and Nelson (1987 and 1989) on the influence of significant others on female entrepreneurs.

The women in this study described how they responded when the need for information or problem solving arose: they would call upon someone who is a trusted resource (spouse, business associate, and friend in the business) and get the answer. If that didn't work, the second response would be to hire a subject matter expert. Every woman in this study described how she relied on someone else's assistance as they are confronted with a business-related problem. These people had been supportive in the past and there was (and there continues to be) a considerable amount of trust and belief in the competence of the one providing advice. The women who relied on their husbands made numerous references to the fact that their husbands had been "career managers" or trained as experts in their own right. Others who were invaluable resources to the entrepreneurial women of this study were people who they had met through their mutual membership in civic, professional, or industry associations. The real estate industry, the personnel services industry, and the construction industry were but three of the groups that provided assistance to the members who were interviewed in the study. One of the women was a member of an Executive group of other company presidents who serve almost as a "Board of Directors" for each other and act as a sounding board for their members. The ability to call on these resources when one needed assistance was highly appreciated among the women interviewed. Long distance telephone calls to ask a question was not a deterrent; what was really valued was that the person being called could be depended upon to provide genuine, honest assistance, based on that person's experience in the business. Again, the personal links with others as sources of expert knowledge was a commonly described phenomenon.

Getting a manual or a textbook and going at it alone is just not the *modus operandi*. Pre-planning does not exist. Spear and Mocker (in Candy, 1991, p. 170) found this to be true in the learners they studied. The women in this study could be classified as "autodidactic learners," that is, learners who engage in an individual, invisible, noninstitutional learning endeavors (Candy, 1991). They experience Spear and Mocker's (1984) "organizing circumstance," the stimulus for their learning. However, long-term learning projects that are organized and deliberate are not the methodology for learning in this group. One woman talked about how she had considered taking a college class to learn about more about accounting, but decided against it because it would take too long.

There is very little reliance on formal education resources or public seminars as described by these women. They believe that education is not a necessary criterion for success: their own experience proves they can be successful without it. About half of the women discussed reading periodicals as a method to gain information; two of the women shared recent readings with me.

Research Question 4: How do they describe their learning?

What the women in this study described was a pattern of learning which started in their childhood years. This learning occurred through the rewards and recognition of those closest to them and through the jobs they held and relationships they formed. The women recounted multiple examples of how learning about themselves has an impact on their organizations and their communities.

With respect to leading their organizations, the self-described leadership roles of these entrepreneurs included sharing their visions of the future with their staff, developing teams and participation in their organizations, leading quality initiatives, and maintaining effective customer relations. They acknowledged that developing trust and support in the people they work with is an essential leadership skill and they believe they know how to do this. They support collaboration and collective problem solving, and keeping people informed (and, moreover, were eager to show me company newsletters and other vehicles for company communication).

The women all talked about relying on their own interpersonal skills to ensure that the structure of the organization is working smoothly. Even the entrepreneur who admitted that her organization had serious employee problems talked about bringing each employee into her office and using her personal influence to encourage them to work more collaboratively and efficiently.

Organizational practices as described by the women indicate that the women of the study would advocate the team management (9,9) style of leadership (Blake and Mouton, 1964) in that they believe in utilizing the skills of committed team members through relationships of trust and respect. Practice of leadership in this group includes team meetings, developing common goals, sharing with others, developing the task skills of employees to better meet the market demands, rewarding creativity and innovation, and encouraging the family connections of employees. Evidences of team-related processes are apparent as one visits the work places of these entrepreneurs. Charts and posters highlighting team performance, company newsletters, gainsharing programs, and continued team training demonstrate a prevalent belief in a team centered leadership style being practiced by these women. The attitudes that the female entrepreneurs in this study expressed regarding learning are that one learns by experience and common sense, that they learn all the time, that they can learn from others, and that they need to continue to learn because their world is changing. The women in this research support the models of adult education in that learning is a lifelong process, and that they are owners of their learning. They also see themselves as facilitators and catalysts in the learning of others.

Research Question 5: What factors affect their learning?

An inner belief in personal power had been developed in these women from childhood and had been reinforced in their work experiences. They had developed a self-image of being different, of being special, of being strong, and of being self-reliant. They had learned these lessons through their interactions with others. And they would apply this image of self and the belief that they were capable of succeeding at anything to the startup of their own businesses.

The entrepreneurs in this study closely resembled the successful entrepreneurs described by David McClelland in his study of male entrepreneurs in India, Malawi, and Ecuador (1987). Like the majority of men in McClelland's study, the majority of these women can be described as proactive, anticipating problems before they were major. They all had high achievement motivation (seizing opportunities, believing that they could do things better than others, demonstrating concern for quality). Numerous statements testified to their high need for achievement. And they all had a commitment to customer satisfaction as a critical component to their continued success.

Self-concepts of potency and self-efficacy are strongly evident in this group of women, supporting their ability to learn (Candy, 1991) The women in this study displayed the characteristics of self-determinism and self-directedness in their narratives: they determine what they need to know to overcome adversity, they take responsibility for getting the knowledge they need, and they engage in critical reflection to determine meaning of the happenings around them. They are self-directed in their learning, as described by Knowles (1975), for they take the initiative to learn and find the answers. Their acquisition of learning involves others but they start the process themselves and, like the popular television advertisement for athletic shoes, they just do it.

ADDITIONAL FINDINGS

One important aspect of learning discussed by almost every woman in this study is the belief that, as successful women, they have a duty and responsibility to improve the work world of other women. They believe that they can share what they have learned and help other women to, perhaps, not have to go through some of their trials and tribulations. These are not strident feminists, clamoring to help their "sisters." These are executive women who believe that they have much to contribute to the development and growth of women in the business world.

Through mentoring, providing technical assistance, and creating informal networks with other women, several of the women of this study are actively providing assistance to other women and do their part in improving the development of women. They are developing new links, new relationships. Hence, these women view themselves not as just being recipients of learning through others, but that they can continue the circle by sharing.

Another avenue for contributing to the benefit of others, used by the women entrepreneurs interviewed in this study, are community action organizations (such as Goodwill and the Boy Scouts). Volunteering to help others is very much a part of the sharing dimension. As such, these women are leaders as described by Astin and Leland (1991): catalysts and facilitators, enabling others to act collectively toward a common goal.

CONCLUSIONS

This research explored how a select group of female entrepreneurs engage in adult learning: what and how they learn and what resources they utilize, and if they fit the model of self-directed learner identified in the adult education literature. Specific interest was directed at discovering if these women engage in learning to acquire leadership skills. That learning is a natural and on-going process in adulthood was a guiding proposition for this research.

The women in this study engage in learning that focuses on two principal areas. The first is that they are continually learning about themselves and defining their self-image. This is a process that started in their childhoods and has resulted in an enhanced belief in their own uniqueness and ability to succeed. They have developed an enhanced sense of personal mastery and confidence that they have the ability to overcome adversity.

The second area of identifiable learning is in the area of business acumen. This group of women described learning endeavors that assisted them in solving business-related problems. When these women needed information to help them in their businesses, this necessitated their taking action to learn. This instrumental learning helped them get a task done and often would involve learning about accounting, franchising, or some legal issue.

The women in this study learned through their relationships with others and by being connected with others. The "others" of influence was often a family member, a significant other (i.e. a mentor or friend), or business associate who is involved in the learning process. The learning was reinforced by positive feedback and on-going support for the woman. As the women described experiences where they learned about themselves, they usually spoke of that learning in the context of another person with whom she had shared an experience. These women do not learn in isolation; they learn with others and from others.

The importance of other people as being resources for these entrepreneurs is reflected in how often they rely on them for assistance. The women spoke of calling upon spouses, close business friends from previous employment, and friends and associates with whom they conduct business today as sources of information. The nature of the learning is unplanned, spontaneous, and informal, truly just-in-time. There is little reliance on formal education processes as resources for learning. As such, these women are very much like the self-directed learner described by

Knowles (1972, 1975). These women are directed into their learning endeavors by their own initiative. They identify their own sources for learning and pursue their quest for information on their own, but relying on others for the answers. Although they do learn through their relationships, they are the drivers of their learning. The way these women learn is definitely assisted by others but these women are accountable to themselves for learning what they believe they need to know and for making the choice as to the resources they will utilize for their learning.

With the exception of one woman, the women in this study would fall into the category of Constructed Knower (Belenky, et al). These entrepreneurs certainly spoke to who they were in the context of their past and present. They have integrated various roles (mothers, wives, sisters, businesswomen, churchgoer, student, community activist, and mentor) without feeling that they had to give one up for another. They believe in the integration of family into the work life of people. They demonstrated a strong sense of caring for other people--their employees, other women, and the community at large. Several women spoke of trying to achieve balance in their lives.

The women in this study demonstrated excitement about learning ("you never get too old to learn," " the more I learn, the more I realize that there are things I want to learn about"). They view new experiences as opportunities to learn.

IMPLICATIONS OF THIS STUDY

The findings of this study have implications for the areas of women's development and leadership development. The women in this study describe a model of learning that is based on the integration of personal experience and the establishment of significant connections and relationships with others. Through this blend, these women have developed a strong sense of their abilities. They have learned how to turn adversity into opportunity by applying their personal power and determination. And they have learned how to be successful as leaders in their businesses.

Following current models of feminine leadership (Helgesen, 1991, Astin and Leland, 1991, Rosener, 1990), the importance of building collaboration and connectedness is a critical skill. The women in this study described how they built relationships with others as a vital part of their learning experiences. They have learned to lead by integrating and sifting through the learnings of their experiences and by developing relationships. They have learned to establish links with others in associations, networks, and mentoring projects that assist them when they need support. They have learned how to build collaboration and cooperation with others.   This research, thus, supports the models of feminine leadership.

It is not just to these models of "women's ways of leading" that this study has relevance. The models of leadership proposed by Kouzes and Posner (1987), Blake and Mouton (1964 and 1985) and Hersey and Blanchard (1969) stress the importance of providing support for people and for being able to build relationships.   Leadership development programs based on these models attempt to develop the people-oriented behaviors of leaders and managers (as well as the task-related skills).   If successful women have learned the relationship building skills as a part of their development (as the women in this study have), they may have an advantage in learning how to lead.   This leads to the question: are they successful because they have learned the relationship-building skills and utilize them effectively?   In today's climate of participative organizational cultures, the women who have learned how to build strong relationship skills from childhood may be better leaders than their male counterparts who are not as adept at building relationships and staying connected with other people.

This study focused on the practices of women who are successful entrepreneurs.   What about those who are starting their businesses or perhaps have not had the same type of background as the women who participated in this study?   Future studies may investigate the differences between successful women and those who are not as successful to determine any differences in how they learn.

Those who are involved with developing curricula for executive and entrepreneurial development for women may want to explore experiences, which capitalize on the learning inherent in relationships, and life experiences of the participants.   This may include developing structured processes to reflect on experience and connections and the value they have contributed to the woman's interpersonal growth. This approach is supported in the findings of the Benchmarks© studies of the Center for Creative Leadership, conducted in the early 1980's. These studies have found that interpersonal skills (i.e. setting a developmental climate for employees, encouraging, developing shared expectations, developing a team, treating others with compassion, sensitivity, and integrity, and the ability to build cooperative relationships) are essential for an executive's success. Developmental strategies for women who wish to improve their leadership effectiveness could include focusing on those experiences which have provided them the most opportunity to develop their interpersonal skills ("lessons learned") and planning strategies for creating new connections with others. Mentoring programs and any networks that encourage a more formalized affiliative learning process would fit the learning styles of women.

Given that the women in this study strongly supported sharing their knowledge with others, they (and other successful entrepreneurs) constitute a vital, energetic resource for other women who need encouragement and support in the business community and others who needed assistance through community involvement organizations.

IMPLICATIONS FOR FUTURE STUDY

Future study in the following areas would further contribute to the fields of adult learning, women's ways of leading, and entrepreneurial studies by increasing what is known about female entrepreneurs:

- An examination of the practice of leadership of successful female entrepreneurs from the perspective of their organizational members to determine how closely aligned self-perception is with organizational perception.
- Research that explores differences between successful and unsuccessful entrepreneurs.
- Research that examines the interpersonal dimensions of a group of successful women entrepreneurs through the use of instrumentation such as Fundamentals of Interpersonal Relationships Inventory (FIRO-B)
- Research that examines the relationship between personality dimensions such as the Myers-Briggs Type Indicator and successful leadership in entrepreneurial organizations.
- Research that tracks a group of female entrepreneurs at inception of their business and monitors actual practices longitudinally.
- Research exploring partnership between successful entrepreneur mentors and fledgling entrepreneur protégés.
- Research which explores the behavioral practices demonstrated by successful male entrepreneurs and successful female entrepreneurs.
- Research which examines, longitudinally, the effects of developing school curricula for girls and boys that reinforces strong self esteem and relationship building skills for both.

Appendices

APPENDIX A: DESCRIPTION OF THE WOMEN PARTICIPANTS OF THIS STUDY

The following is a description of each of the women who participated in this study, presented in the order of the interviews. The women's names are presented as pseudonyms.

Interview One: Georgia Roberts

Georgia Roberts is the owner of a retail store specializing in products that provide relief to sore backs. This is her second entrepreneurial venture. Georgia grew up in Florida: her father was a professor at the University of Florida and her mother was a homemaker. She had started businesses as early as age five when she had a small soda fountain. Later endeavors included selling magazines door to door and starting a day camp for small children, an activity that won her acclaim in *Seventeen* magazine.

Not having completed college, Georgia worked as a legal secretary to support her husband through graduate school. She came to Texas with one child in tow when her husband accepted a teaching position at the University of Texas. Georgia was then 28 and she decided that she no longer wanted to work for anyone else. She borrowed $3,000 from two faculty member friends and started a copying service. The copying business grew and Georgia ran her business until health problems at age 40 necessitated her selling it--and Georgia became a millionairess. Her health improved, she traveled around the world for several years, and she returned to Austin looking for a new project. Her entrepreneurial interests led her to develop the back product store and its expansion through franchises throughout the United States.

Georgia wears her salt-and-pepper hair cut around her face and she wears glasses, which she is prone to peer over the top of from time to time. At our meeting, she wore low-heeled shoes and a comfortable-looking dress and light jacket. She gives the impression that attention to fashion is not a significant part of her life. Before I left her offices, Georgia demonstrated how some of her products work on my back and she invited me to come up to her store. I did visit the store within the week and saw Georgia there, leading a couple of potential franchisees through the store. She greeted me and expressed her pleasure at seeing me there.

Interview Two: Beth Cole Milne

I had heard Beth Cole Milne speak at an Austin Women's Chamber of Commerce meeting where she spoke on her experiences as an entrepreneur. She owns a large, full-service beauty services business which employs over 35 service providers and generates over $1 million in revenues yearly. Beth had been in the beauty services business all of her working life, starting smaller salons and continuously growing until she had reached her current organization structure. Beth had grown up on a farm near a small town in eastern Texas, graduated from high school in 1957, and moved to Austin. She always had an interest in the beauty business, patterning herself after an adored aunt who had a salon in Houston. Diminutive in stature, Beth wears her almost white-blond hair short and fashionable. In her fifties, she wore a trendy outfit on the day of our interview, as she had the evening she spoke to the women's group.

Beth's communication style is immediately warm and personal. During our interview, I felt as if we had known each other a long time and that we were just "catching up" on old news. Beth uses her hands expressively and leans forward as she talks, engrossed in the conversation.

Beth has been engaged in personal development work as a way to explore the spiritual dimension of her work. She studied Werner Erhardt and became involved as an instructor with a group, which does energy and personal mastery training. At the time of our interview, she was heavily involved with implementing a total quality initiative in her company that included personal awareness training for each of her employees. She was also applying for a grant to the New Quality College (loosely affiliated with Dr. Deming) in Hammond, Louisiana to develop a curriculum for quality in service organizations.

Beth and I met at a cafe located around the corner from her business establishment. She owns the old home converted into a three-floor salon in a fashionable section of Austin. One is struck by the contrast of entering a beautiful old home (dating from the 1800's) with its leaded glass doors and, once inside, finding an elaborate computer system which handles appointments and provider schedules, documents customer records and maintains inventory controls. Beth has combined New Age with High Tech and created a highly successful business.

Interview Three: Paula Goodman

Paula Goodman met with me at her offices in a condominium office park late one afternoon. Her offices were full of people waiting for interviews with the recruiters who work for her, for Paula owns an employment services company and a temporary employment service. Paula instructed her secretary to hold all calls and we had our meeting in her office. Her office is a moderately-sized room, reminiscent of a home office. There is color on the walls, desk and table lamps, a sofa and easy chair for one-to-one discussions, a large desk, and flowers and plants tastefully situated. Several plaques and awards were on the walls, as was a bookshelf full of books and binders. Framed pictures of her children were prominently displayed on an end table.

Paula was dressed in a red tailored dress and high heels, with her hair neatly coifed, very much the picture of a corporate executive. She was poised and relaxed through our meeting, sitting on the sofa.

Currently in her forties, Paula was married to an executive for the telephone company. During their years together, they had moved many times. She had not graduated from college, having left prior to finishing to get married. She had worked as a pre-school assistant, a substitute teacher, and had stayed home for several years raising their two children. When her husband was transferred to Austin, she and he decided to look for a business to buy for her to run as a way to earn the money to support their children's college education. In 1981, they bought an employment agency of which she became the President and shortly thereafter, she started the temporary services agency. She runs them both today. Because Paula's husband had had over twenty-five years' experience as an executive, she relied heavily on his expertise at the start of her business. His influence has diminished over the years, as she believes that she has grown tremendously through the years in her role. Her companies employ ten full-time recruiters, secretarial staff, and varying numbers of temporary employees who are found temporary assignments and are paid through her service.

Paula is involved with several community organizations, the most notable one dedicated to helping middle schoolers stay in school. She professes strong Christian beliefs and maintains that her company has been successful due to her commitment to integrity, fairness, common sense, and doing what is right. One of her mottoes: do to one as you would have them do unto you.

Interview Four: Dana Johnson

Real estate has been a fundamental part of Dana Johnson's family history. Her father was a developer, so she grew up with real estate. She attended the University of Texas at Austin, thinking she would study medicine. After three years at the university, she left at the age of 20 and opened a commercial research office for a major real estate firm entering the Austin market. She went free lance about a year later and did research, brochure work, and syndications for commercial real estate companies. In 1980, she bought the Austin franchise for a large national real estate firm and went into full service. Shortly after that, she married a man who had been in real estate development. Each of them owns several companies, which form six complementary corporations. Her largest company employs 250 people with four offices in Austin.

At 44, Dana looks very much the executive. She is polished and articulate in her conversation and presented herself confidently. She was neatly attired in a business suit, with her hair pulled back with a headband, and cosmetics modestly applied. Our meeting lasted about ninety minutes and during that time, Dana had an opportunity to introduce me to her husband and to show me the layouts for a new relocation brochure she was developing for her company.

Interview Five: Lil Kohler

Lil Kohler grew up on a farm in Tennessee. Her first jobs included picking cotton and milking cows. She left school when she was fifteen and in the ninth grade to get married. At eighteen, she left Tennessee for Dallas, she was separated from her husband, and she was seeking employment to support herself and her children. She was able to gain employment at a yearbook publishing company and quickly was selected to be group team leader. After four years and the acquisition of a GED, Lil went to work on the manufacturing line at Texas Instruments. Here again, she excelled: when the average raise was three cents an hour and an exceptional raise was six cents, Lil received fifteen cents an hour increase as her first raise. She became a group leader in one year, became the first woman in engineering in the company, and in 1968, started the Chip Sales department, an entrepreneurial group which became the most profitable division in the company.

For a hobby, while still a division manager at TI, Lil got involved with selling home decorating products and became the seventh in her sales district of 900 representatives. She debated going into the multi-level marketing program full time when she was asked to be the general manager for a new company in California. She accepted the position, partly for the increase in salary, partly for the increased challenge, and partly for the experience it would provide for her children, who had never been out of Grand Grand Prairie, Texas, a Dallas suburb. Four years later, after growing the new company into a fourteen million-dollar concern, and after successfully battling melanoma, Lil decided to leave the company over a conflict in values between the owner and herself.

At that point, Lil then decided to start her own company--and called upon her former associations at TI for support. She moved her company from Los Angeles to Austin, married a Georgetown University professor who had assisted her relocation effort, and reached nine million dollars in sales the third year of operation. Lil's company currently employs 150 employees (team members) and she utilizes a participative approach in managing the company. Her daughter is Human Resources Director and her son is President (Chief Executive Officer). Lil's company has been recognized for its innovations and accomplishments in the Quality area; she implemented a gainsharing program for her employees and has started a school for her employees' children.

Lil is tall, slender, and looks younger than her 56 years. The day of our interview, she wore her long dark hair in a full ponytail and she was hobbling around in a cast and crutches. It had only been a few days since she broke her ankle: she had been doing early morning aerobics in her hotel room on a business trip. Full of energy, Lil continued her appointments' schedule after she visited the hospital in Boston!

Interview Six: Marta Garza

Marta Garza, general contractor and president of a commercial construction company, responded favorably to my telephone request for an interview. We were to meet in a local cafe one Saturday morning in July. I arrived early and was surprised to have a petite, dark-haired woman with flowing curls dressed in shorts and a ruffled blouse come over and introduce herself. This was certainly a differently attired person than the one I had seen photos of: a woman with a hard hat, jeans, and clunky worker boots. This woman was boldly dressed, confident in her stride, and she looked younger than her 46 years of age.

Marta had been born and raised near McAllen, Texas, a small town in the Rio Grande Valley. Fourth of nine children, her father worked in a lumberyard and her mother was a homemaker. Marta was very close to her family and had accompanied her father on his delivery rounds. She did well in school, especially in English. One of her first jobs was to tutor a Spanish exchange student at her school. She graduated from high school in 1967 and entered college studying English and history. After three years in college, she withdrew to assist her family after the untimely death of her father. Shortly thereafter, she married a young man who was a manager with the telephone company. Her first experience at a building project was to construct their first house when they moved to San Antonio. As her husband made career moves, she accompanied him--and would construct a new house. They relocated to Austin in 1978 and Marta went to work with a couple of women who remodeled homes. Marta loved working outdoors and completing the projects. The two women decided to leave the house remodeling business, but Marta decided she wanted to learn more and she loved the construction industry. She then took a job working as the secretary/administrative assistant for a builder. She learned all aspects of the business: payroll, keeping project management schedules, dealing with subcontractors.

Marta left her job with the builder after making a decision to bid on a project herself. She did not have insurance or any of the administrative systems of a new construction business in place. But when she won the bid, she immediately went right to work to get her business off the ground. She claimed that she was eager and that she was not lazy. She has built commercial buildings throughout Austin (including the fire station that services my neighborhood).

Marta is still married to the same telephone company executive and they have one daughter in her teens. A women-in-construction group has cited her for her achievements as a minority contractor.

Interview Seven: Cammy Hargrove

Cammy Hargrove grew up in Austin. She owns and operates a traffic sign and barricade company. Cammy is in her forties, has one child and is married to a man who works in the manufacturing and purchasing departments of her company. A tall woman, she speaks softly and thoughtfully, as if she considers every word before saying it.

Prior to her becoming active in a business that supports the street construction and repair industry, Cammy had worked in clerical positions for the state government and had stayed at home with her daughter. She reentered the work force when her daughter reached school age. She went to work in her parents' business because it afforded her work schedule flexibility. Cammy became more involved in her parents' barricade business until 1982, when she started her own sign business. Five years later, having lost one parent and dealing with poor health of the other, Cammy merged both the businesses into one large company and became president of the merged organization. She employs eighty people and feels responsible for their well being and that of their families. She feels responsible to keep them working.

Cammy's company primarily subcontracts to highway contractors, although she believes that a lot of the problems associated with subcontracting and dealing through others would be eliminated if her business could competitively bid directly with the city or state to develop traffic control plans. Most of the highway contractors she deals with are men; dealing with the "good old boy network" is part of doing business in her industry. Cammy's strategy to deal with the men has been to hire a man to do the interface.

The morning I met with Cammy, I drove over to her corporate offices in north Austin. Her offices are located at the end of a street, behind chain link fences, in two prefab-type buildings surrounded by all sorts of traffic barricade signs. Cammy's executive office looked somewhat out of place in the context of the forklifts and barricades outside: she had oil paintings, Queen Anne style office furniture, and flowers in her office. Cammy had photos of her child and sister's children on her bookcase. Our meeting lasted approximately sixty-five minutes; Cammy suggested two other women for me to consider for inclusion in the study.

Interview Eight: Ann Mills

Ann Mills is the youngest entrepreneur in the study for she is in her early thirties. She grew up in Massachusetts with a brother and her mother, a behavioral psychologist who finished her graduate work while Ann was an adolescent. Ann claimed that her mom did a lot of research at home! Ann's father had been an executive in a major computer company, also in Massachusetts. Her parents were depression children and had a strong work ethic, which Ann feels, transferred to her.

Among Ann's work experiences was a stint as the youngest employee hired at an Arby's roast beef and working as a waitress. She attended Tufts University, majoring in pre-med, and started working to pay for her living expenses as a freshman. She worked throughout her college years at an ice cream store. That experience led her to post-college employment, opening restaurants and ice cream stores for the owners, putting aside her plans for medical school. She had proved herself to be competent: at 21, she opened an ice cream store in Manhattan, handling all functions from talking with architects to opening the doors on the first day. Ann decided to open her own business when the owners of the company decided to sell to a Burger King multi-unit operator and the upper management of the organization deteriorated the work of the local management. Ann had read about the growth potential of Austin, Texas, so she visited and met with local business development leaders, and then she decided to move to the Central Texas hill country. Ann currently has retail stores throughout Austin and sells ice cream in the local supermarkets. She is expanding into Houston.

Ann and I met in her office, above the first store she had opened in Austin. Her office was full of creative artwork of paper mache and construction paper. I found out that these are applications for employment--applicants are asked to put together something that describes their favorite ice cream. Ann is a slight woman with long dark hair that she wears loose over her shoulders. It is hard to imagine her in a boxing ring but she is a professional woman boxer (at 110 pounds), a sport she took up after she found marathon running was too hard on her back. She especially likes boxing because it is a much-misunderstood thinking sport.

Interview Nine: B.T. King

Cammy Hargrove suggested that I meet with B.T. King, the owner of a company that designs and manufactures slip ring assemblies. I called B.T. and she agreed to participate. I met B.T. at her office one morning; she had been writing out her Christmas cards before I arrived. B.T.'s office walls were full of pictures of her daughters and a picture of a young man and a steer he had raised and had sold to B.T. through the local 4H.

B.T. grew up in the Houston area, raised by a widowed father and her paternal grandmother. She grew up during the depression and did not go to college. Instead, she married her husband at the age of 18. After World Wars and living on a farm, they moved to Austin and started their business.

B.T. has run her company for the last twenty years. She had been working with her husband in the slip ring business for about ten years prior to his retiring and leaving her the chief executive role. Her daughter and son-in-law are in senior management positions, and B.T. anticipates leaving the business to them when her health prohibits her from continuing in the senior leadership role.

Her company consists of twenty-five employees, many of whom have worked with B.T. for the last ten to fifteen years. She truly runs the company as a large family. Much of our interview consisted of B.T. talking to me about the employees and how much she relies on them for their help and support. After our interview, I met every employee and had an opportunity to chat with some of them. B.T. is like everyone's grandmother. She knows every employee's personal and family history; in fact, some employees have a spouse or a child who have worked in the company. Prior to my leaving B.T.'s facility, she presented me with fresh pecans from her ranch.

Interview Ten: Eliza Brady

Eliza Brady came from a small Southern town. After high school, she attended a college but did not have any career aspirations. She dropped out of college at nineteen, went to California, met and married a fellow Texan, and started raising a family. The marriage fell apart when she was 24; Eliza subsequently started looking for employment to support herself and her two children. After jobs working as a waitress and as a secretary in an architect's office, Eliza returned with her children to Texas. She gained employment at a copying service and became the owner's right hand person. When the owner could not manage the company any longer, Eliza pulled together a buyout. She then become the President of the company and has led the company through successful expansion.

Eliza is in her mid-forties, very stylish in her attire. She has been President of her Rotary Club and is active in community Quality programs. She has remarried and is involved with personal growth projects: she is taking violin lessons and plays in a country music band and she also takes singing lessons. Her goals include staying with her company for another three years or so and then taking a less active role in its management. She feels that making choices about how much she wants to her business to thrive allows her to maintain balance in her life.

Interview Eleven: Judy Gage

Judy Gage owns a plumbing, air conditioning and heating business in Northwest Austin. Her offices are in a converted home with plenty of parking space behind the building for the many trucks in her business fleet.

Judy had agreed to meet with me after I heard her speak at a Women's Chamber of Commerce meeting. She is a friendly person who is easy to speak to--our meeting lasted almost two hours. Judy grew up in Kansas. She told me that her parents were just teenagers trying to grow up when they had her; they had not completed high school. She worked as a teenager to buy clothes and books for school and, although she did go to college for a year, she dropped out to get married and support her husband through school. She worked in a bank as a branch manager until she was 28, gaining experience in a small customer-focused establishment. She divorced her first husband and married a man who had been a bank customer and who, incidentally, owns a sister company to Judy's company in Florida. This couple commutes long distance on weekends to spend time together and with their son.

Judy's business grosses $5 million each year with 97 employees. She is quite involved with building teams in her work force and enabling more participation among her employees. Judy is involved with an Executive Group which she claims acts like a Board of Directors, a group to which she can go with problems and get advice. She is also very active with lobbying in support of and protecting small businesses.

Interview Twelve: Kay Soma

Kay Soma is the president of an advertising and public relations firm in San Antonio. She had been raised in Alabama and came to Texas with a degree in Political Science. She had taught in the San Antonio school system until she asked for maternity leave and was told that she would not return to being a Social Studies teacher. At first she was told there wouldn't be any position; the school district rethought its position and offered her job teaching Special Education, something she was not prepared to do. Kay made a major move, took her retirement money out of the system and went to work for the Boy Scouts in the Exploring Division. At that position, she met the head of an advertising firm. He offered her a position doing political advertising. She accepted and later wound up leaving the company several years later due to her impending marriage to that man. At that point she started her own company.

Kay's organization is small with just ten people, but it offers employees who are interested in learning all aspects of advertising and the opportunity to learn the business. Her clients have recognized her for her innovativeness. Kay is busy training her employees in team and group dynamics and integrating Total Quality principles in their work.

The morning we met, Kay and I had breakfast in a small cafe near her offices in downtown San Antonio. She wore non-corporate clothes: jeans, a T-shirt and a sweatshirt around her shoulders. She is a slender woman in her forties who gets excited when talking about how she has overcome challenges, when talking about future opportunities, and when talking about her horse. Kay was awarded "Entrepreneur of the Year for 1993" in San Antonio.

Interview Thirteen: Kate Hammond

Kate Hammond owns and is the president of a software development company in Austin. She is in her late forties and, prior to starting on the path that led her to her current position, had been a linguistics professor at a university in the Northwest. Newly divorced, with two small children, Kate decided that she needed to enter a field with more earning potential than university teaching. She took a sabbatical and, with Ph.D. in hand, studied computer programming for a year. She then went to work for Texas Instruments and became immersed in the world of software development. From that firm, she went to a research consortium that explores applications for software. Kate developed her idea for a company while at the research consortium and later spearheaded the consortium's first "spinout" company. Her company is only two years old and it is having success in tailoring specialized software programs for specific customer needs. Kate has been awarded "Entrepreneur of the Year for 1993" in Austin.

Interview Fourteen: Maria Garcia

One Saturday morning, I drove down to San Antonio and met with Maria Garcia, the president of an office supply company. A slight woman with medium-length hair and glasses, she had asked to meet me at her own modern office building in an industrial park south of the San Antonio airport. Entering her office suites, I noted a large poster of a thermometer on the wall (the rising temperature equaling rising sales). Maria's personal office walls were literally covered with plaques of accolades from the Small Business Administration, "Who's Who" organizations, and the City of San Antonio.

Maria has been in business since 1973, having started as an 18-year-old with an office supply inventory she purchased on the spur of the moment for $1,500. The second of five children, Maria was born in Monterrey, Mexico and came to the United States as a youngster. Her father was a laborer on dairy farms, and her mother has been a homemaker. Her early years as an entrepreneur were full of hardship: door to door sales, a building roof falling into her inventory, a car accident which destroyed her only means of transportation, and an IRS fine for tax reporting errors made by her CPA. Maria has overcome every obstacle with determination and spirit. Her main competition at this time comes from the large discount office suppliers who have a "superstore" approach to selling. In an effort to meet the competition, Maria had entered the computer supplies and custom application field; this has not been as successful as she wanted so she is looking at other areas into which to diversify. Maria is also exploring alternative rewards systems for her staff.

Maria has not married; she maintains close ties with her family. She admitted in our interview that she had had no time to get married. She related how, in the early days of her company, she had to work part time at selling mobile homes to support herself. She is very active in the Mexican American Unity Council and the Goodwill Industries board, among others.

Interview Fifteen: Belinda Watkins

Belinda Watkins owns an electronics business that supplies two-way radios and other electronic equipment, a field that she loves because it is constantly changing. It is also a field where there are few women, something which didn't intimidate Belinda when she started her business in 1976 at the age of 24. She had been raised to feel that there were no fields designated for women or for men.

Belinda, the oldest of four children, was raised in south Texas: her father was an engineer who had worked on the Apollo capsules and her mother was a certified lab technician. Her father passed away when she was twelve and her mother is currently enrolled in school studying sociology and gerontology. Belinda did not complete college, although she studied social sciences and psychology when she was enrolled.

Belinda presents a picture of a strong, confident woman. Her handshake is firm, she has a ready smile, and she uses her height (5'11") as a strength. During our meeting, she laughed at how men often appear to be intimidated by her being tall, expecting, perhaps, that she be sweet, demure, and dressed in ladylike frills. Belinda has had experience in challenging male-dominated systems: she sued the City of Austin for violation in contracting procedures. In fact, she spent her life savings doing so. Her guiding credo through the whole process was "I just kept hearing, 'you can't do this and you can't do this' and I'd spent my whole life being told that you can't do this and I've done it." Belinda was successful in her fight with the city.

Belinda is involved with a small business initiative to provide counseling and business help for women entrepreneurs. She is a volunteer fire woman in the small town where she lives, south of Austin.

Interview Sixteen: Caren Thomas

I met Caren Thomas at seven a.m. for coffee at a cafe where she is a regular customer with her business meetings. Seated a table away were the current and newly-elected presidents of the local Austin Chamber of Commerce. They greeted Caren warmly, for she had been the last year's president of the same organization and they all work closely for the continued business success of the city.

Caren is in her late forties. The day of our meeting, she was smartly dressed in a business suit, heels, and her short hair neatly framing her face. She exudes a sense of energy and vitality: her step is lively and quick.

Caren grew up in Massachusetts. Her father was a machinist who always had a second job to put the children through school; her mother taught grade school. Caren's formal schooling was conducted at Cornell Nursing school. She had worked as a nurse at an Indian reservation in California while accompanying her husband on his Air Force assignment. A subsequent move brought the family to Austin in the 1970's and, Caren, when faced with lower wages for nurses, decided to expand a side-line business of selling Hummels and collectibles. The need to create a system for inventorying her products led her to discover the world of computers and the assistance data processing could provide her business. That discovery opened a door of opportunity for Caren: in 1979, she opened a computer sales store in Austin that was a remarkable success. She had forty-four full time employees, ten part time and she did over $12 million in sales. Later, she opened a computer rental business as well. In 1985, she sold the business, continuing to operate it as the president.

Caren's current business endeavors capitalize on the business connections she has made through the years. She is linking businesses together in partnership arrangements that are mutually beneficial (i.e. small business owners with venture capitalists).

Caren is often asked to speak at local college commencements and graduate school programs, she is on an advisory board for the Federal Reserve, she has testified in Congress on initiatives for Small Businesses and she is still active with the local Chamber. She has dedicated a part of her life to assisting women who are just starting out in the business world through a group mentoring process. Her children grown, she starts each day with a four-mile walk and is focusing on keeping balance in her life.

Interview Seventeen: Karen Lewis

Karen Lewis started and operates a steel rebar business in San Antonio. With no college degree, her first job was working as a bookkeeper in the metal services industry. Through jobs with different employers, she acquired the information needed to run her own business that she started in 1985. Her first office was in her kitchen, where she worked steel trades by telephone. Since 1991, she has occupied a prefab building in a somewhat isolated area off the interstate in northeast San Antonio with fifty employees.

The Saturday that we met, Karen and an assistant were working at her offices. She was trying to sort out a serious problem caused by transferring all her company inventory and billing to a computer system, which incorrectly tracked the data. Further, the vendor of the software system, in an effort to "fix" the problem, exacerbated the situation. Karen was determined to remedy the situation herself, even if it meant working each weekend and at night to solve the computer glitch.

Karen's business is facing tremendous challenges from large international steel conglomerates, which are entering the local markets, and causing pricing wars. This trickles down to the small rebar firms which must cut overhead costs in order to remain competitive. For Karen, maintaining reasonable overhead costs will decide whether she can sustain her business. This influences the compensation system for employees and the type of people who will work in the steelyard. Karen's employees are not skilled and she spoke to me of the problems she experiences with her work force. At the time of our interview, Karen was overwhelmed with internal vandalism and a less-than-committed workforce. She believes that if she becomes personally involved with her employees, she can influence them to work more productively.

Karen has considered moving into another field which is less dependent on low overhead or perhaps downsizing her organization to a more manageable size; however, she enjoys and knows the steel rebar business. Karen is in her fifties and one of her two sons works with her in her business.

Interview Eighteen: Lisa Bollcher

Lisa Bollcher is an entrepreneur based in San Antonio and her business consists of selling and servicing telephone headsets for industries which are involved in customer sales and service (i.e. airline reservations agents, insurance company customer service representatives). Lisa's business career started as a bookkeeper for a heating and air conditioning business, followed by a move into civil service, and a stint as a real estate agent. It was during the depressed housing market of the '80's that she decided to go back to college and get a degree in business administration. She was a single mom with two children and decided that she needed to increase her earning ability in a stable field. Lisa met her second husband while in school. They formed a cleaning supply company together in San Antonio; the communications supply business is her second entrepreneurial endeavor.

Lisa is in her fifties, a diminutive woman with short salt and pepper colored hair. Her husband works with her in her business as do her two children. One of the challenges facing Lisa at this time is the strategic plan for her company and trying to decide a succession plan for herself. During our lunchtime interview, she told me that she has a couple of new businesses in mind and that she is interested in writing fiction. In fact, she had already written a short story that she might submit to a magazine for possible publication.

APPENDIX B:
DEMOGRAPHICS OF THE WOMEN PARTICIPANTS

Interview Order # Assigned to Interviewee

	1	2	3	4	5	6	7	8	9	10	11	12	13	14	15	16	17	18
Family Background																		
Blue Collar/Agrarian		x			x	x		x			x	x	x		x	x	x	x
Professional	x		x	x			x		x	x				x				
Birth Order	1	2	5	2	1	4	2	1	3	3	4	1	1	1	1	4	2	2
Age																		
30's							x											
40's			x	x		x			x	x	x	x	x	x	x	x	x	x
50's	x	x			x													
60's																		
70's								x										
Ethnicity																		
Nonminority	x	x	x	x	x		x	x	x	x	x	x	x		x	x	x	x
Hispanic						x								x				
Education Level																		
High School/GED		x			x			x						x			x	
Some College			x	x		x	x			x	x				x			
Bachelor's	x											x				x		x
Advanced Degree									x				x					
Vocational		x			x													
Marital Status																		
Single							x								x	x		
Married w/Children		x	x		x	x		x	x	x	x	x	x	x			x	x
Married w/o Children				x														
Divorced w/children	x																	
Family Involvement																		
Spouse in Business			x			x												
Children in Business	x	x			x			x									x	x

APPENDIX C:

INTERVIEW GUIDE

Entrepreneur's Name:_____

Interview Location_____

Date/Time:_____

Ethnicity:_____

Age:_____ Education Level:_____

Interview Question 1: How did you get to your current position as CEO/President of your organization?

_____

_____

_____

Interview Question 2: What do you do in your current role as the head of this organization?_____

_____

_____

_____

_____

Notes:_____

_____

_____

_____

_____

_____

_____

_____

_____

_____

_____

APPENDIX D: CATEGORIZING

The following are Lincoln and Guba's (1985) operational steps for categorization through comparison of units of information for a single analyst. These steps bring together into provisional categories those cards that apparently relate to the same content; to devise rules that describe category properties and that can, ultimately, be used to justify the inclusion of each card that remains assigned to the category as well as to provide a basis for later tests of replicability; and to render the category set internally consistent.

1. Given the pile of cards that has resulted from the unitizing process, and that will be more or less haphazardly arranged, select the first card from the pile, read it, and note its contents. This first card represents the first entry in the first yet-to-be-named category. Place it to one side.

2. Select the second card, read it, and note its contents. Make a determination on tacit or intuitive grounds whether this second card is a "look-alike" or "feel-alike" with Card 1, that is, whether its contents are "essentially" similar. If so, place the second card with the first and proceed to the third card; if not, the second card represents the first entry in the second yet-to-be-named category.

3. Continue on with successive cards. For each card decide whether it is a "look/feel-alike" of cards that have already been placed in some provisional category or whether it represents a new category. Proceed accordingly.

4. After some cards have been processed, the analyst may feel that a new card neither fits any of the provisionally established categories nor seems to form a new category. Other cards may now also be recognized as possibly irrelevant to the developing set. These cards should be placed in a miscellaneous pile; they should not be discarded at this point, but should be retained for later review.

As the process continues in this fashion, new categories will emerge rapidly at first, but the rate of emergence will diminish sharply after some fifty to sixty cards have been processed. At this point certain of the "look/feel-alike" categories will have accumulated a substantial number of cards, say, six to eight, and the analyst may begin to feel pressed to start on the memo-writing task leading to the delineation of category properties and devising of a covering rule. Proceed:

5. Take up cards that have accumulated in such critical-size categories. Make an effort to put into a prepositional statement the

properties that seem to characterize the residue of cards. Combine these properties into a rule for inclusion. Write the provisional rule on another index card and place it immediately adjacent to the category. Give the category a name or title that catches as well as possible the "essence" of the rule, to make it easier in later sorting to note quickly the content of each category. When the rule has been provisionally established, review each of the cards in the category to be sure that their inclusion can be justified on the basis of the rule. Some cards may be discarded into the miscellaneous pile, or form the nucleus for a new category. In some cases this review will lead to an immediate revision of the rule itself, to accommodate the included cards in a more satisfactory way. The analyst should be on the watch for anomalies, conflicts, or other inadequacies that require attention.

6. Continue with steps 3 and 4 above, and with step 5 as other categories approach critical size, until the cards have been exhausted. Whenever a card is now assigned to a category for which a provisional rule has been devised, the card should be included or excluded not on the basis of its "look/feel-alike" quality but on the basis of its fit to the rule. Anomalies, conflicts, and other inadequacies may become evident as this step proceeds, and must be dealt with as indicated in step 5. If such problems are dealt with by rule revision, cards assigned to the category on the basis of the earlier rule formation must be reviewed to be certain that they still "belong."

7. When the pile of unit cards has been exhausted, the entry category set should be reviewed. First, attention should be given to the cards assigned to the "miscellaneous" pile. Now that the full category set is apparent it may be the case that cards labeled as miscellaneous during early stages of the categorization process may be seen to fit in somewhere after all. Some cards may be judged to be clearly irrelevant and may be discarded. Others may remain unresolved, no clear-cut decision about them apparently possible. As a rule of thumb, these unassignable (but not discardable) cards ought not to exceed more than 5 to 7 percent of the total; a percentage in excess of that figure signals a serious deficiency in the category set.

Second, the categories themselves should be reviewed for overlap. The set is inadequate if there are ambiguities about how any particular card might have been categorized. Some unit cards may have been prepared inappropriately in the first place, bearing dual content. In such cases, the cards should be rewritten onto two cards so that unambiguous assignments can be made. Categorization can be accomplished most cleanly when the categories are defined in such a way that they are internally as homogeneous as possible and externally as heterogeneous as possible. The analyst should check for that characteristic.

Third, the set of categories should be examined for possible relationships among categories. It is possible that certain categories may be subsumable under others; that some categories are unwieldy and should be further subdivided; and/or that some categories are missing, a fact made evident by the logic of the category system (or some subportion of it) as a whole. For example, if the category system has a subset of cards dealing with various aspects of affording parents of handicapped children due process in developing IEP'S (individual educational programs), it would be immediately evident, say, if no cards were included that described the appeal process to which aggrieved parents might have recourse. Further, other categories may be incomplete, showing sufficient presence to have been included but no sufficient to be definitely established. Missing, incomplete, or otherwise unsatisfactory categories should be earmarked for follow-up as part of the continuous data collection/processing sequence. (pages 347-349)

APPENDIX E: CATEGORIES WHICH AROSE OUT OF INTERVIEW DATA

Category 1: Demographics
Rules for Inclusion: Birth order, Family size, Family financial background, Family educational background, Education level

Category 2: Childhood Experiences
Rules for Inclusion: Significant events remembered as contributing to their development, Mentor or sponsor as growing up, Someone who paid attention to them, Childhood business ventures

Category 3: Relationships
Rules for Inclusion: Significant other, Spouse, Family (including children), Father, Mother, Aunt, Friends, Previous Employers, Mentors, Investors

Category 4: Business Startup
Rules for Inclusion: Types of previous work experience, Events in previous experience which led to starting own business, Support to start business

Category 5: Crisis/Barriers to Business
Rules for Inclusion: Looking at problems as opportunities

Category 6: Personal Goals
Rules for Inclusion: Personal lifetime goals, Measures of success

Category 7: Knowledge of Self
Rules for Inclusion: Personal power, Sense of being different or unique, Positive feedback for being different or unique than peers, When knew wanted to be in business, Personal competency in chosen field, Practice of critical reflection, Self-examination: identifying personal strengths and weaknesses, Faith in one's ability to "Make it work"

Category 8: Personal Values
   Rules for Inclusion: Religious orientation, importance of spiritual dimension of life, Strong sense of values, personal ethics, integrity, Implanting of values as a child, Building a business using their values to guide them

Category 9: What These Women Do as Leaders (Roles/Responsibilities)
   Rules for Inclusion: Focus the organization on goals, Create a vision and share it, Crisis management, Making decisions, Keeping on top of "new" trends that will help the business (i.e. quality), serving as a link with others outside the organization, Developing new business, Keeping priorities in line, Being a team builder, Providing support to employees, Being a content knowledge source of support for their organization, Setting an ethical standard

Category 10: Awareness of Learning Needs
   Rules for Inclusion: How they know they need more knowledge, Need to learn more about marketing, Need to learn more about automation/data processing/computer systems, Need to learn more about planning

Category 11: What/ How They Acquire New Information/Learn
   Rules for Inclusion: What is learned, Just-in-Time Nature of the learning, Formal Industry-sponsored classes, Evening classes, College programs designed for working adult students, Seminars , Assistance from others (Spouse with corporate-learned experience, Personal friends in the industry, Others who have worked in the industry hired in to be a knowledge source employee in the organization, Professional sources, i.e., lawyers, accountants, Friends/ acquaintances, Mentor in organization of which they may have been a member), Personal reading (Books, Magazines)

Category 12: Impact on Others
   Rules for Inclusion: Being appreciated by employees, Being appreciated/valued by customers, Sharing in Community, Formal organizational or association membership, Sense of "owing" or paying back to society, Credibility for their industry by working for betterment of the community

APPENDIX F: RELATIONSHIP OF UNITS OF ANALYSIS AND INTERVIEW CATEGORIES

Interview Order (# assigned to each interviewee)

Categories	1	2	3	4	5	6	7	8	9	10	11	12	13	14	15	16	17	18
Demographics																		
Birth Order	x	x	x	x	x	x	x	x	x	x	x	x	x	x	x	x		x
Family Size	x	x	x	x	x	x	x	x	x	x	x	x	x	x	x	x		x
Family Fin. Background	x	x	x	x	x	x	x	x	x	x	x		x	x	x	x		x
Family Educ Bkgrnd	x	x	x	x	x	x	x	x	x	x	x		x	x	x	x	x	x
Education Level	x	x	x	x	x	x	x	x	x	x	x	x	x	x	x	x	x	x
Childhood Experiences																		
Significant Events	x	x	x	x	x	x	x	x	x	x	x	x		x	x	x		x
Mentor or Sponsor	x		x	x	x	x	x											x
Someone paid attention	x	x		x	x	x	x	x	x		x	x	x	x	x			x
Childhood bus.ventures	x			x	x		x	x	x		x	x			x	x		x
Relationships																		
Significant Other	x	x		x	x	x	x	x	x	x	x	x	x	x	x	x	x	x
Spouse			x	x	x	x		x	x	x		x				x	x	x
Family (children)	x				x	x		x	x	x	x	x				x	x	x
Father, Mother, Aunt	x	x				x	x	x	x	x			x	x	x	x	x	x
Friends	x		x	x	x	x	x	x	x	x	x	x	x	x	x	x	x	x
Previous Employers	x		x	x	x	x		x			x	x	x	x	x	x	x	x
Mentors, Investors	x			x		x			x		x			x				
Business Startup																		
Types Prev. Work Exp.	x	x	x	x	x	x	x	x	x	x	x	x	x	x	x	x	x	x
EventsPrev.Work Exp.	x	x	x	x	x	x	x	x	x	x	x	x	x	x	x	x	x	x
Support to start business	x		x	x	x	x		x	x	x	x	x	x	x	x	x	x	x
Barriers to Opportunities																		
Problems=opportunities	x	x	x	x	x	x	x	x	x	x	x	x		x	x			x

APPENDIX F: RELATIONSHIP OF UNITS OF ANALYSIS AND INTERVIEW CATEGORIES

Categories	Interview Order (# assigned to each interviewee)																	
	1	2	3	4	5	6	7	8	9	10	11	12	13	14	15	16	17	18
Knowledge of Self																		
Personal Power	x	x	x	x	x	x	x	x	x	x	x	x	x	x	x	x		x
Sense of being different	x	x	x	x	x	x	x	x	x	x	x	x	x	x	x	x		x
Positive Fdbck from others	x	x	x	x	x	x	x	x	x	x	x	x	x	x	x	x		
Knew wanted to be in bus.	x	x	x	x	x	x	x	x	x		x	x	x	x	x	x	x	x
Personal competency	x	x	x	x	x	x	x	x	x	x	x	x	x	x	x	x		x
Practice of critical reflectio	x	x		x	x		x		x		x		x	x	x			
Self-examination	x	x	x	x	x		x		x	x		x						
Faith in self to succeed	x	x	x	x	x	x	x	x	x	x	x	x	x	x	x		x	x
Roles/Responsibilities																		
Focus org. on goals	x	x	x	x	x		x	x	x	x	x	x	x	x	x	x	x	x
Create a vision & share	x	x	x	x	x	x		x	x	x	x	x	x	x	x	x		x
Crisis management	x		x	x		x		x	x	x	x		x				x	x
Decision making	x	x	x	x	x	x	x	x	x	x	x	x	x					
Keeping on top of trends	x		x	x	x	x	x	x		x	x			x	x			x
External Link	x		x	x		x	x		x	x	x	x	x	x	x	x	x	x
Developing new business	x	x	x	x	x	x	x	x	x	x	x	x	x	x	x	x	x	x
Prioritizing		x		x	x		x	x		x	x	x	x				x	x
Team Building		x	x	x	x	x	x	x	x	x	x	x	x	x	x	x	x	x
Support to Employees	x	x	x	x	x	x	x	x	x	x	x	x	x				x	x
Setting an ethical standard	x	x	x		x	x	x	x	x	x	x	x	x	x	x	x	x	x
Awareness of Learning Needs																		
How they know they need	x	x	x	x	x	x	x	x	x	x	x	x	x		x	x	x	x
Marketing	x			x		x		x									x	x
Automation/dp systems			x	x													x	x
Planning		x		x	x	x	x	x	x		x	x				x	x	x

APPENDIX F: RELATIONSHIP OF UNITS OF ANALYSIS AND INTERVIEW CATEGORIES

Categories	Interview Order (# assigned to each interviewee)																	
	1	2	3	4	5	6	7	8	9	10	11	12	13	14	15	16	17	18
What/How They Learn																		
What is learned	x	x	x	x	x	x	x	x	x	x	x	x	x	x	x	x	x	x
JIT nature of learning	x		x	x	x	x	x	x	x	x	x	x	x	x	x	x	x	x
Industry sponsored classes		x	x	x		x		x		x								
Evening Classes	x													x	x			
College programs	x	x					x							x		x		x
Seminars	x	x		x		x		x			x			x	x	x		x
Assistance from others	x	x	x	x	x	x	x	x	x	x	x	x	x	x	x	x	x	x
Personal Reading		x	x	x	x		x	x		x	x	x		x	x	x		x
Pers Growth Activities	x	x		x	x		x		x	x	x	x	x	x	x			x
Imp. of Spiritual Dimension																		
Strong sense of values	x	x	x	x	x	x	x	x	x	x	x	x	x	x	x	x	x	x
Personal Ethics	x	x	x	x	x	x	x	x	x	x	x	x	x	x	x	x	x	x
Integrity	x	x	x	x	x	x	x	x	x	x	x	x	x	x	x	x	x	x
Implanting of Values	x	x	x	x	x	x	x	x	x	x	x	x	x	x	x			x
Building bus.w/values	x	x	x	x	x	x	x	x	x	x	x	x	x	x	x	x	x	x
Personal Goals																		
Personal Lifetime Goals	x	x	x	x		x	x	x		x	x	x	x	x	x	x	x	x
Measures of Success		x	x	x	x	x		x	x	x	x	x	x	x	x	x	x	x
Impact on others																		
Appreciated/employees	x	x		x		x	x	x	x	x	x	x	x		x			
Appreciated by customers		x	x	x	x	x	x	x	x	x	x	x	x	x	x			x
Sharing in Community	x	x	x	x	x	x	x	x	x	x	x	x	x	x	x	x		
Association Membership		x	x		x	x		x	x	x				x	x	x	x	x
Giving back to society	x	x	x		x	x	x	x						x	x	x		
Betterment of community			x	x	x	x	x	x	x	x	x			x	x	x	x	x

Bibliography

Acker, Joan, Barry, Kate, and Esseveld, Johanna (1991). Objectivity and Truth: Problems in Doing Feminist Research. In Fonow, Mary Margaret and Cook, Judith A. (Ed.) *Beyond Methodology, Feminist Scholarship as Lived Research*. Bloomington: Indiana University Press.

Adenuga, Babatunde O. (1989). *Self-Directed Learning Readiness and Learning Style Preferences of Adult Learners*. Dissertation, Iowa State University.

Anderson, Carl R., and Schneier, Craig Eric.(1978). Locus of Control, Leader Behavior and Leader Performance Among Management Students. *Academy of Management Journal*, Vol. 21, No. 4, 690-698.

Anderson, Lynn R. and McLenigan, Margaret (1987). Sex Differences in the Relationship Between Self-Monitoring and Leader Behavior. *Small Group Behavior*, Vol. 18(2) pp. 147-167.

Andrisani, P.J., and Nestel, G.(1976). Internal-External Control as Contributor to and Outcome of Work Experience. *Journal of Applied Psychology*, Vol.61.

Argyris, C. and Schon, D.A. (1974). *Theory in Practice: Increasing Professional Effectiveness*. San Francisco: Jossey Bass.

Arlin, Marshall, and Whitley, Theodore W. (1978). Perceptions of Self-Managed Learning Opportunties and Academic Locus of Control: A Causal Interpretation. *Journal of Educational Psychology*, Vol. 70, No. 6, 988-992.

Astin, Helen S., and Leland, Carole (1991). *Women of Influence, Women of Vision*. San Francisco: Jossey-Bass.

Bailey, Kenneth D. (1978). *Methods of Social Research*. New York: The Free Press.

Bandura, Albert (1977). *Social Learning Theory*. Englewood Cliffs, NJ: Prentice-Hall.

Baraka-Love, J.N. (1986). *Successful Women: A Racial Comparison of Variables Contributing to Socialization and Leadership Development*. UMI Dissertation: Western Michigan University.

Barrentine, Pat (ed.) (1993). *When the Canary Stops Singing: Women's Perspectives on Transforming Business*. San Francisco: Berrett-Koehler.

Bart, Barbara D. (1983). Educational Interests of Small Business. *Journal of Business Education*, Nov. pp. 82-85.

Baumol, W.J. (1983). Toward Operational Models of Entrepreneurship. In Ronen, J. (ed) *Entrepreneurship*. Lexington: D.C. Heath.

Belcourt, Monica. (1990). A Family Portrait of Canada's Most Successful Female Entrepreneurs. *Journal of Business Ethics*, Vol. 9 (4-5), p. 435.

Belenky, M.F., Clinchy, B.M., Goldberger, N. R., and Tarule, J.M. (1986). *Women's Ways of Knowing, The Development of Self, Voice, and Mind.* New York: Basic Books.

Bennis, Warren, and Nanus, Burt (1985). *Leaders.* New York: Harper & Row.

Bennis, Warren (1989). *Why Leaders Can't Lead.* San Francisco: Jossey-Bass.

Bing, Sandra Kay (1990). *The Relationship of the Leader Behavior and the Skills for Excellence of Women in Higher Education Administration.* UMI Dissertation: West Virginia University.

Birley, Sue (1989). Female Entrepreneurs: Are They Really Any Different? *Journal of Small Business Management*, Vol. 27 (1).

Birley, Sue, Moss, Caroline, and Saunders, Peter (1987). Do Women Entrepreneurs Require Different Training? *American Journal of Small Business* 12 (1), pp. 27-35.

Blake, Robert R. and Mouton, Jane S. (1964). *The Managerial Grid.* Houston, TX: Gulf Publishing Company.

Blake, Robert R. and Mouton, Jane S. (1986). *Executive Achievement.* Houston, TX: Gulf Publishing Company.

Bogdan, Robert C. and Biklen, Sari Knopp (1982). *Qualitative Research for Education: An Introduction to Theory and Methods.* Boston, MA: Allyn & Bacon, Inc.

Bowen, Donald D. and Hisrich, Robert D. (1986). The Female Entrepreneur: A Career Development Perspective. *Academy of Management Review*, Vol.11 (2).

Brockett, R.G., and Hiemstra, R. (1991). *Self-Direction in Adult Learning: Perspectives on Theory, Research, and Practice.* London and New York: Routledge & Kegan Paul.

Brookfield, S.D. (1986). *Understanding and Facilitating Adult Learning.* San Francisco, CA: Jossey-Bass.

Brookfield, S. (1984). Self-directed Adult Learning: A Critical Paradigm. *Adult Education Quarterly*, Vol. 35, No. 2, pp. 59-71.

Bruner, Jerome (1966). *Toward a Theory of Instruction.* Cambridge, MA: Harvard University Press.

Bruner, Jerome (1978). *The Process of Education*, 2d ed. Cambridge, MA: Harvard University Press.

Caffarella, Rosemary S.(1992). *Psychosocial Development of Women: Linkages to Teaching and Leadership in Adult Education.* Columbus, OH: ERIC Clearinghouse on Adult, Career, and Vocational Education, Ohio State University.

Caffarella, Rosemary S., and O'Donnell, Judith M., (1987). Self-Directed Adult Learning: A Critical Paradigm Revisited. *Adult Education Quarterly*, Vol. 37, No. 4.

Callender, Willard D. (1992). Adult Education as Self-Education. *Adult Education Quarterly*, Vol. 42, No. 3.

Candy, Philip C. (1991). *Self-Direction for Lifelong Learning, A Comprehensive Guide to Theory and Practice.* San Francisco, CA: Jossey-Bass.

Carsrud, Alan L., Gaglio, Connie Marie, and Olm, Kenneth W. (1987). Entrepreneurs: Mentors, Networks, and Successful New Venture Development: An Exploratory Study. *American Journal of Small Business*, Vol. 12 (2). pp.13-18.

Chaganti, R. (1986). Management in Women-Owned Enterprises. *Journal of Small Business Management*, October, pp. 18-29.

Chene, Adele (1983). The Concept of Autonomy in Adult Education: A Philosophical Discussion. *Adult Education Quarterly*, Vol. 34(1) pp. 38-47.

Chodorow, N. (1971). Family Structure and Feminine Personality. In *Women, Culture and Society*, M.Z. Rosaldo and L. Lamphere, Ed. Stanford, CA: Stanford University Press.

Cohen, R.S. and Lefkowitz, I. (1977). Self-esteem, Locus of Control and Task Difficulty as Determinants of Task Performance. *Journal of Vocational Behavior,*11, 314-32.

Collins, Orvis, and Moore, David (1970). *The Organization Makers.* New York: Appleton Century Crofts.

Cotterill, Pamela and Letherby, Gayle (1993). Weaving Stories: Personal Auto/Biographies in Feminist Research. *Sociology*, Vol. 27, No. 1, pp. 67-79.

Cross, K.P. (1981). *Adults as Learners.* San Francisco: Jossey-Bass.

Cuba, Richard, Decenzo, David, and Anish, Andrea (1983). Management Practices of Successful Female Business Owners. *American Journal of Small Business*, Vol. 7(2), pp. 40-47.

Dechant, Kathleen (1992). Knowing How to Learn: The "Neglected" Management Ability. *Journal of Management Development.* Vol. 9, No. 4, pp.40-49.

Denmark, Florence L. (1977). Styles of Leadership. *Psychology of Women Quarterly.* Vol. 2, No. 2, pp. 99-113.

Diffley, Judy High (1983). Important Business Competencies for the Female Entrepreneur. *Business Education Forum,* April, pp. 31-3.

Drucker, Peter F. (1992). *Managing for the Future: the 1990's and Beyond.* New York, NY: Truman Talley Books/Dutton.

Durand, D.E., and Shea, D.(1974). Entrepreneurial Activity as a Function of Achievement, Motivation, and Reinforcement Control. *The Journal of Psychology,* Vol. 88, pp. 57-63.

Dyer, W. Gibb, (1992). *The Entrepreneurial Experience.* San Francisco, CA: Jossey-Bass.

Eagly, Alice H. and Karau, Steven J. (1991). Gender and the Emergence of Leaders: A Meta-Analysis. *Journal of Personality and Social Psychology,* Vol. 60(5), pp. 685-710.

Ellsworth, Jill H. (1992). Adults' Learning: The Voices of Experience. *Journal of Adult Education,* Vol. 21, No. 1, pp. 23-34.

Feeney, Helen M. (1980). Women's Education. In Boone, Shearon, White and Associates *Serving Personal and Community Needs Through Adult Education.* San Francisco, CA: Jossey-Bass.

Fisher, James C., and Podeschi, Ronald L.(1989). From Lindeman to Knowles: A Change in Vision, *International Journal of Lifelong Education,* Vol. 8. No. 4, pp. 345-353.

Fonow, Mary Margaret and Cook, Judith A. (Ed. 1991). *Beyond Methodology, Feminist Scholarship as Lived Research.* Bloomington: Indiana University Press.

Fried, Lisa I. (1989). A New Breed of Entrepreneur: Women. *Management Review,* Vol. 17 (12) .

Gale, Linda Lyman (1989). Gender and Leadership: The Implications of Small Group Research. *Initiatives.*

Garrison, D. Randy (1987). Self-directed and Distance Learning: Facilitating Self-Directed Learning Beyond the Institutional Setting. *International Journal of Lifelong Education,* Vol. 6(4), pp. 309-315.

Garrison, D.R. (1992). Critical Thinking and Self-directed Learning in Adult Education: An Analysis of Responsibility and Control Issues. *Adult Education Quarterly,* Vol. 42, No. 3.

Glaser, B.G. and Strauss, A.L. (1967). *The Discovery of Grounded Theory: Strategies for Qualitative Research.* Chicago: Aldine.

Goffee, R. and Scase, R. (1985). *Women in Charge: The Experiences of Female Entrepreneurs.* London: George Allen and Unwin.

Goldwasser, Shirley Whiteman (1988). *Competency and Success: A Study of Women Business Leaders.* Dissertation, Georgia State University.

Greiner, L. (1972). Evolution and Revolution as Organizations Grow. *Harvard Business Review*, July-August.

Haas, Howard G. (1992). *The Leader Within*. New York: Harper Business.

Hart, Mechthild U. (1990). Liberation Through Consciousness Raising. In Mezirow and Associates, *Fostering Critical Reflection in Adulthood*. San Francisco: Jossey Bass.

Harvey, J.H., Barnes, R. D., Sperry, D.L. and Harris, B. (1974). Perceived Choice as a Function of Internal-External Locus of Control. *Journal of Personality*, 42, pp. 437-452.

Helgesen, Sally (1990). *The Female Advantage, Women's Ways of Leadership*. New York, NY: Doubleday Currency.

Hersey, Paul and Blanchard, Ken (1969). *Management of Organizational Behavior, Utilitizing Human Resources*. Englewood Cliffs: Prentice Hall.

Hiemstra, Roger (1987). Creating the Future. In *Continuing Education in the Year 2000, New Directions for Continuing Education*, No. 36, Brockett, R.G. ed., San Francisco: Jossey-Bass.

Hisrich, Robert D. (1986). The Woman Entrepreneur: A Comparative Analysis. *Leadership and Organization Development Journal*, Vol. 7(2) pp. 8-16.

Hollander, Edwin P. and Yoder, Jan (1984). Some Issues in Comparing Women and Men as Leaders. In William E. Rosenbach and Robert L. Taylor (Eds.). *Contemporary Issues in Leadership*, Boulder: Westview Press.

Houle, C.O.(1961). *The Inquiring Mind*. Madison, WI: University of Wisconsin Press.

Ibrahim, A.B. and Goodwin, J.R. (1987). Perceived Causes of Success in Small Business. *American Journal of Small Business*, Vol. 3.

Jayaratne, Toby Epstein and Stewart, Abigail G. (1991). Quantitative and Qualitative Methods in the Social Sciences. In Fonow, Mary Margaret and Cook, Judith A. (Ed.) . *Beyond Methodology, Feminist Scholarship as Lived Research*. Bloomington: Indiana University Press.

Joe, V.C. (1971). Review of Internal-External Control Construct as a Personality Variable. *Psychological Reports*, 28, pp. 619-640.

Josselson, R. (1987). *Finding Herself*. San Francisco: Jossey-Bass.

Kanter, Rosabeth Moss (1977). *Men and Women of the Corporation*. New York: Basic Books.

Kerlinger, Fred N. (1986). *Foundations of Behavioral Research*. 3rd ed. Orlando: Holt, Rinehart, and Winston, Inc.

Kirkwood, Catherine (1993). Investing Ourselves: Use of Researcher Personal Response in Feminist Methodology. In de Groot, Joanna and

Maynard, Mary. *Women's Studies in the 1990's.* Hampshire: The Macmillan Press, Ltd.

Knowles, Malcolm (1975). *Self-Directed Learning.* Chicago, Follett Publishing.

Knowles, M.S. (1972). *The Modern Practice of Adult Education: Andragogy versus Pedagogy.* New York: Association.

Knox, A.B. (1977). *Adult Development and Learning: A Handbook on Individual Growth and Competency in the Adult Years.* San Francisco: Jossey-Bass.

Kouzes, James M. and Posner, Barry Z. (1987). *The Leadership Challenge, How to Get Extraordinary Things Done in Organizations.* San Francisco, CA: Jossey-Bass.

Kovalainen, Anne (1988). Toward a New Research Model of Gender in Management and Leadership Studies. *International Journal for the Advancement of Counseling,* 11, pp. 305-312.

Krebs, Bonnie (1988). *The Visibility of Women as Leaders in Opposite-Sex and Mixed-Sex Groups.* UMI Doctoral Dissertation: Columbia University.

Lawrence, Paul R. and Lorsch, Jay W. (1969). *Developing Organizations: Diagnosis and Action.* Reading, MA: Addison-Wesley.

Lefcourt, H.M. (1972). Recent Developments in the Study of Locus of Control. In B.A. Maher (Ed.), *Progress in Experimental Personality Research.* New York: Academic Press.

Lincoln, Yvonna and Guba, Egon (1985). *Naturalistic Inquiry.* Newbury Park CA: Sage.

Lindeman, Eduard C. (1926). *The Meaning of Adult Education.* New York: New Republic Press, Inc.

Lipper III , Arthur (1988). Defining the Win and Thereby Lessening the Losses for Successful Entrepreneurs. *Journal of Creative Behavior,* Vol. 2(3) pp. 172-177.

Livingston, J. Sterling (1971). Myth of the Well-Educated Manager. Reprinted in *Paths Toward Personal Progress: Leaders are Made, Not Born, Harvard Business Review* (1982).

Lofland, John and Lofland, Lyn H. (1984). *Analyzing Social Settings, A Guide to Qualitative Observation and Analysis,* 2nd Ed. Belmont, CA: Wadsworth Publishing.

Lombardo, Michael M. (1984). How Do Leaders Get to Lead? In William E. Rosenbach and Robert L. Taylor (Eds.) *Contemporary Issues in Leadership.* Boulder: Westview Press.

Long, Huey B. (1990). Psychological Control in Self-Directed Learning. *International Journal of Lifelong Education,* Vol. 9(4), pp. 331-338.

Longstreth, Molly, Stafford, Kathryn, and Maudlin, Theresa (1987). Self-Employed Women and Their Families: Time Use and Characteristics. *Journal of Small Business Management*, Vol. 25, No. 3, July.

Luttrell, W. (1989). Working Class Women's Ways of Knowing: Effects of Gender, Race, and Class. *Sociology of Education*, Vol. 62, No. 1, pp. 33-46.

Manz, Charles, and Manz, Karen P. (1991). Strategies for Facilitating Self-Directed Learning: A Process for Enhancing Human Resource Development. *Human Resource Development Quarterly*, Vol.2, No. 1.

Marsick, Victoria J. (1990). Altering the Paradigm for Theory Building and Research in Human Resource Development. *Human Resource Development Quarterly*, Vol. 1, No. 1.

Martin, Patricia Yancey (1992). Feminist Practice in Organizations: Implications for Management. In Fagenson, Ellen A. (Ed.) *Women in Management*. Newbury Park, CA: Sage.

Master, Nancy Briggs (1989). *Leadership Styles and Career Paths of Selected Women in Higher Education Administration and Corporate Administration*. UMI Doctoral Dissertation: University of Nevada, Las Vegas.

McClelland, David C. (1987). Characteristics of Successful Entrepreneurs. *Journal of Creative Behavior*, Vol. 21(3), pp.219-233.

Megargee, E.I.(1969). Influence of Sex Roles on the Manifestation of Leadership. *Journal of Applied Psychology*, Vol. 53, pp. 377-382.

Merriam, Sharan B. and Caffarella, Rosemary S. (1991). *Learning in Adulthood*. San Francisco, CA: Jossey-Bass.

Merriam, S.B. and Clark, C.M. (1991). *Lifelines: Patterns of Work, Love, and Learning in Adulthood*. San Francisco: Jossey-Bass.

Mezirow, J. (1985). Concept and Action in Adult Education. *Adult Education Quarterly*, Vol. 35(3), pp. 142-151.

Mezirow, J., and Associates (1990). *Fostering Critical Reflection in Adulthood: A Guide to Transformative and Emancipatory Education*. San Francisco: Jossey Bass.

Mies, Maria (1991). Women's Research or Feminist Research? The Debate Surrounding Feminist Science and Methodology. In Fonow, Mary Margaret and Cook, Judith A. (Ed.) *Beyond Methodology, Feminist Scholarship as Lived Research*. Bloomington: Indiana University Press.

Mintzberg, Henry (1990). The Manager's Job: Folklore and Fact. *Harvard Business Review*, Vol. 68 (2).

Mishler, Elliot G. (1986). *Research Interviewing, Context and Narrative*. Cambridge, MA: Harvard University Press.

Morgan, Gareth (1988). *Riding the Waves of Change: Developing Managerial Competencies for a Turbulent World.* San Francisco, CA: Jossey-Bass.

Morgan, Gareth and Smircich, Linda (1980). The Case for Qualitative Research. *Academy of Management Review,* Vol.5, No. 4.

Moore, Dorothy P. (1990). An Examination of Present Research on the Female Entrepreneur-Suggested Research Strategies for the 1990's. *Journal of Business Ethics,* Vol. 9.

Morrison, Ann M., White, Randall P., Van Velsor, Ellen, and the Center for Creative Leadership (1992). *Breaking the Glass Ceiling.* Reading, MA: Addison Wesley.

National Women's Business Council (1991). *Annual Report to the President.* Washington, D.C.

Neider, Linda(1987). A Preliminary Investigation of Female Entrepreneurs in Florida. *Journal of Small Business Management,* Vol. 25 (3).

Nelson, Debra L. and Quick, James C. (1985). Professional Women: Are Distress and Disease Inevitable? *The Academy of Management Review,* Vol.10 No. 2.

Nelson, George W. (1989). Factors of Friendship: Relevance of Significant Others to Female Business Owners. *Entrepreneurship: Theory and Practice,* Vol. 13(4).

Nelson, George W. (1987). Information Needs of Female Entrepreneurs. *Journal of Small Business Management,* Vol. 25(3).

Noe, Raymond (1988). Women and Mentoring: A Review and Research Agenda. *Academy of Management Review,* Vol.13 (1), pp. 65-78.

Oakley, Ann (1981). Interviewing Women: A Contradiction in Terms. In Roberts, H. (ed). *Doing Feminist Research.* New York: Routledge.

Oddi, Lorys F., Ellis, Alice J., and Roberson, Jean E. Altman (1990). Construct Validation of the ODDI Continuing Learning Inventory. *Adult Education Quarterly,* Vol. 40, No. 3, pp. 139-145.

Peck, T.A. (1986). Women's Self-Definition in Adulthood: From a Different Model? *Psychology of Women Quarterly,* Vol. 10, No. 3, pp. 274-284.

Penland, P. (1979). Self-initiated Learning. *Adult Education,* 29, pp. 170-179.

Peters, T. (1990). The Best New Managers will Listen, Motivate, Support. Isn't That Just Like a Woman? *Working Woman,* pp. 142-217.

Peters, T.J. and Waterman, R.H. Jr. (1982). *In Search of Excellence: Lessons from America's Best-Run Companies.* New York: Harper & Row.

Phares, E.J. (1968). Differential Utilization of Information as a Function of Internal-External Control. *Journal of Personality,* 36, pp. 649-662.

Phares, E.J. (1976). *Locus of Control in Personality.* Morristown, N.J.: General Learning Press.

Pinson, Linda and Jinnett, Jerry (1992). *The Woman Entrepreneur.* Tustin, CA: Out of Your Mind and into the Marketplace Publishers.

Pratt, D.D. (1988). Andragogy as a Relational Construct. *Adult Education Quarterly,* Vol. 38(3), pp. 160-181.

Riding, Allan L. and Swift, Catherine S. (1990). Women Business Owners and Terms of Credit: Some Empirical Findings of the Canadian Experience. *Journal of Business Venturing,* Vol. 5 (5), pp.327-340.

Rogers, Carl R. (1961). *On Becoming a Person.* Boston: Houghton Mifflin.

Rogers, Carl R. (1983). *Freedom to Learn for the 80's.* 2d edition, New York: Merrill, Macmillan Publishing Company.

Rosener, Judy B. (1990). Ways Women Lead. *Harvard Business Review,* Vol. 68(6).

Rossing, Boyd E.(1991). Patterns of Informal Incidental Learning: Insights from Community Action. *International Journal of Lifelong Education,* Vol. 10, No. 1, pp. 45-60.

Rotter, J.B. (1966). Generalized Expectancies for Internal Versus External Locus of Control of Reinforcement. *Psychological Monographs* 80, (1,WholeNo.609).

Roueche, John E., Baker, George A. III, Rose, Robert R. (1989). *Shared Vision: Transformational Leadership in American Community Colleges.* Washington, D.C.: Community College Press.

Russell, Joyce E.A., Rush, Michael C., and Herd, Ann M. (1988). An Exploration of Women's Expectations of Effective Male and Female Leadership. *Sex Roles,* Vol.18(5-6), pp. 279-287.

Rymell, R.G. (1981). *Learning Projects Pursued by Adult Degreed Engineers.* Unpublished doctoral dissertation. University of North Texas.

Sayles, Leonard R. (1993). *The Working Leader: The Triumph of High Performance Over Conventional Management Principles.* New York: MacMillan.

Scase, R. and Goffee, R. (1982). Why Some Women Decide to Become Their Own Bosses. *New Society,* Sept. 9.

Scase, Richard, Goffee, Robert, and Mann, Anna (1987). Women Managers. *Management Today,* March.

Scherer, Robert F., Brodzinski, James D., and Wiebe, Frank A. (1990). Entrepreneurial Career Selection and Gender: A Socialization Approach. *Journal of Small Business Management,* Vol. 28, (2).

Schwartz, Eleanor Brantley (1976). Entrepreneurship: A New Female Frontier. *Journal of Contemporary Business,* Winter. pp. 47-76.

Schumpeter, J.A. (1961). *The Theory of Economic Development*. New York: Oxford University Press.

Scott, Carole E. (1986).Why More Women Are Becoming Entrepreneurs. *Journal of Small Business Management*, Vol. 24 (4) pp.37-43.

Smith, Ken G. and Gannon, Martin J. (1987). Organizational Effectiveness in Entrepreneurial and Professionally Managed Firms. *Journal of Small Business Management*, Vol. 25, pp.14-18.

Smith, Mary Lee (1987). Publishing Qualitative Research. *American Educational Research Journal*, Vol. 24, No.2, pp. 173-183.

Solomon, George T. and Winslow, Erik K. (1988). Toward a Descriptive Profile of the Entrepreneur. *Journal of Creative Behavior*, Vol. 22(3), pp. 162-171.

Solomon, George T. and Winslow, Erick K. (1989). Further Development of a Descriptive Profile of Entrepreneurs. *Journal of Creative Behavior*, Vol. 23(3), pp. 149-161.

Spear, George E. and Mocker, Donald W. (1984). The Organizing Circumstance: Environmental Determinants in Self-Directed Learning. *Adult Education Quarterly*, Vol. 35, No. 1.

Spindler, George and Louise (1970). Fieldwork Among the Menomini. In G.D. Spindler (Ed.), *Being an Anthropologist, Fieldwork in Eleven Cultures*. New York: Holt Rinehart, and Winston.

Stevenson, Lois A. (1986). Against All Odds: The Entrepreneurship of Women. *Journal of Small Business Management*, Vol. 24(4), pp. 30-36.

Stevenson, Lois A. (1990). Some Methodological Problems Associated with Researching Women Entrepreneurs. *Journal of Business Ethics*, Vol.9.

Steward, James F., and Boyd, Daniel R. (1988). Teaching Entrepreneurs: Opportunities for Women and Minorities. *Business Forum*, Vol. 13 (3).

Stodgill, R.M. (1974). *Handbook of Leadership*. New York: Free Press.

Stoner, Charles R., Hartman, Richard I., and Arora, Raj (1990). Work-Home Role Conflict in Female Owners of Small Businesses: An Exploratory Study. *Journal of Small Business Management*, Vol. 28 (1).

Tannenbaum, Robert and Schmidt, Warren H. (1973). How to Choose a Leadership Pattern. Reprinted in *Paths Toward Personal Progress: Leaders are Made, Not Born, Harvard Business Review*. (1982)

Tavris, Carol (1992). *The Mismeasure of Woman*. New York: Simon and Schuster.

Taynor, J. and K. Deaux, (1974). When Women are More Deserving than Men: Equity, Attribution, and Perceived Sex Differences. *Journal of Personality and Social Psychology.* Vol. 28, pp.360-367.

Tough, A.M. (1967). *Learning Without a Teacher: A Study of Tasks and Assistance During Adult Self-Teaching Projects.* Educational Research Series, No. 3. Toronto: Ontario Institute for Studies in Education.

U.S. Department of Commerce, Bureau of the Census (1990). *Women-Owned Business, 1987.* Washington, D.C.: U.S. Government Printing Office.

U.S. Presidential Report (1979). *The Bottom Line: Unequal Enterprise in America.* Washington, D.C.: U.S. Government Printing Office.

Van Velsor, Ellen and Hughes, Martha W. (1990). Gender Differences in the Development of Managers: How Women Managers Learn from Experience. *Center for Creative Leadership Technical Report No. 145.*

Wilkens, Paul H. (1979*). Entrepreneurship-A Comparative and Historical Study.* New Jersey: Ablex Publishing Corp.

Winslow, Erik K. and Solomon, George T. (1989). Further Development of a Descriptive Profile of Entrepreneurs. *Journal of Creative Behavior.* Vol.22 (3), pp.149-161.

Yin, Robert K. (1989). *Case Study Research, Design and Methods.* Newbury Park, CA: Sage.

Zeithaml, Carl P. and Rice, George H. (1987). Entrepreneurship/Small Business Education in American Universities. *Journal of Small Business Management,* Vol.12(1), pp. 44-50.

Index

www.ingramcontent.com/pod-product-compliance
Ingram Content Group UK Ltd.
Pitfield, Milton Keynes, MK11 3LW, UK
UKHW020413010325
455677UK00029B/879